EATING
EGGLESS

EATING
EGGLESS

Cooking and Living Creatively with an Allergy to Eggs

Elizabeth Moody Campbell

Published by Haida Point Property LLC, Seattle, WA
www.eatingeggless.com

Edited and Designed by Girl Friday Productions
www.girlfridayproductions.com
Editorial: Meghan Harvey, Emilie Sandoz-Voyer, Lisa Gordanier, and Em Gale
Interior Design: Paul Barrett
Cover Design: Todd Bates
Logo Concept: Angela Turk Art & Design
Cover Images and Food Photography © Lindsey Denman

ISBN-13: 978-0-692-56264-2
ISBN-10: 0-692-56264-8
eISBN: 978-0-692-56263-5

First Edition

Printed in the United States of America

In memory of my mother, who started me on my journey to creative eggless cooking and taught me how to live with asthma and food allergies.

All proceeds will go to support food allergy education and research at Health and Science Education Outreach at Seattle Children's Research Institute.

EDUCATION IS KEY . . .

Whether we are parents or educators, restaurant owners or coaches, we all have a role to play in keeping people who have food allergies safe. Through education we can learn how to reduce the risk of exposure to allergens, how to recognize the symptoms of an allergic reaction, and how to work together to create a safe and welcoming environment for people with food allergies.

Amanda L. Jones, PhD
Director, Health and Science Education Outreach
Seattle Children's Research Institute

CONTENTS

INTRODUCTION

Eating Eggless presents creative recipes to be enjoyed by everyone, and especially by those with an allergy to eggs or who generally wish to avoid eggs. Because I have been allergic to eggs all my life, cooking without them has become second nature to me.

The purpose of this book is to give the reader many helpful suggestions for eating out, grocery shopping, and traveling, as well as to provide a selection of time-tested recipes for many occasions. These have been enjoyed by family and friends through the years. Many tips are listed in Eight Steps to Eating the Eggless Way, and the resource section provides helpful information on such subjects as where you might encounter hidden eggs and what to substitute for eggs. Each recipe chapter begins with a section called Tips and Hints for preparing food from that chapter, and all through the book Egg Alerts and Cook's Notes pop up in appropriate places.

A number of the recipes are suitable for vegetarians or could be made so with a little variation. Most recipes are my originals or were recreated from wonderful family and friends' recipes as well as from published books. Since you surely have your own favorite recipes, I suggest ways to make them eggless without making major changes to the ingredient list.

Fifteen million Americans have food allergies, and that includes approximately three million children. Although only about 1 percent of all Americans have an allergy to eggs, it is the second-most-common food allergy for young children. I was motivated to write a book that covered just egg allergies, rather than including additional allergens, because I wanted to share my recipes and knowledge about living with an egg allergy so others could live with the least amount of restrictions.

As I grew up, my mother created many eggless dishes—especially desserts and cookies. Her creative ways inspired me to continue developing new recipes to follow some of the food trends of today. *Eating Eggless* is intended to be a stepping stone for those with an egg allergy, so they can cook and eat out with a new and safer vision for eating without eggs.

Every recipe in *Eating Eggless* uses readily available food products, so be adventuresome with your cooking, and as you gain confidence, you'll be able to convert your own favorite recipes to versions that taste delicious *and* contribute to your long-lasting health and happiness.

Bon Appétit!

EIGHT STEPS TO EATING THE EGGLESS WAY

1. READ, READ, READ!

- Packaged food ingredients change without notice, so it is very important to read the ingredient list every time you purchase a product or even select a different size package of the same brand.
- Shopping for food with your new knowledge about your food allergy will take longer, but the time you spend reading labels will save you from suffering later. For example, would you suspect egg yolk to be an ingredient in plain bottled horseradish?
- If you have just recently become allergic to eggs, take a little time to read recipes you see in books and magazines to familiarize yourself with the many ways eggs are added to foods. It makes eating away from home easier when you know where eggs could possibly be lurking.
- It's better to be safe than sorry: Read the label before you purchase the product. Read the label when you put the product in the cupboard, and read the label again when you use the product for the first time. It is so easy to miss that little three-letter word!

BE VIGILANT ABOUT READING LABELS

2. HIDDEN EGGS

- When contemplating eating something you haven't prepared, if you are not sure of the ingredients, DO NOT EAT IT. It is so easy to think a food served to you should not contain eggs, but don't guess. Check Resources and Information for a list of common food products that contain hidden eggs (page 223).
- Eggs and egg by-products also go by many different names. See Resources and Information for a list of manufacturers' names for these products (page 227).

- Cholesterol-lowering egg substitutes sold in the dairy section of the supermarket contain egg whites and should NOT be used for egg-free cooking.
- Some drugs and vaccinations contain small amounts of egg product. Check with your health-care provider before you receive any inoculations or other medications, and confirm that your allergy is noted on your medical records. Double check with your pharmacist as well.

PREVENTION—ASK BEFORE YOU EAT!

3. CROSS CONTAMINATION

- Be on the lookout for cross contamination, as one or several small pieces of food you are allergic to could accidently fall into the food being prepared for you. Cutting boards, salad bowls, grills, and woks are all common sources of cross contamination. It can happen in a restaurant as well as in a friend's kitchen. It can also take place in your home kitchen if others in your household eat eggs or use products that contain eggs.

- Restaurants may cook eggless pasta in the same kettle of water used to cook egg pasta or slice vegetables on the same board that was used to slice eggs. Ask your server to have your food prepared in an area free from eggs and for the preparer to use clean gloves.

- One of the most common points of cross contamination is in the area of sandwich preparation, as mayonnaise (which is typically made with eggs) is so frequently used. Clearly specify that you do not want mayonnaise or other "special sauces" that may contain mayonnaise. Peek under the bread when it is served to double check.

- At large functions, salads are often premade, so it is an easy practice for the kitchen staff to lift the egg off the salad and serve it as egg-free. Ask to have a new salad made for you, as fragments of the egg may remain on your lettuce.

- In bakeries, eggless items may share a tray, work surface, or pan with other foods that contain egg. Be safe and enjoy home baking or labeled packaged foods.

- At salad bars and delis, serving utensils are often unintentionally shared between the various containers, so look carefully at all serving spoons, forks, and tongs. Also, crumbles of egg may fall into neighboring containers. It is best to avoid food that is one or two trays on either side of the eggs.

BE A DETECTIVE AND BE WATCHFUL

4. EATING WITH FRIENDS
AT THEIR HOME OR YOURS

- When you are invited to a friend's home for a meal, be up front and mention that you or your child has an allergy to eggs or other foods, but that you do not want them to vary their menu because of you. If they mention a food that would normally contain eggs, offer to bring your own substitute. You will then know you can eat safely. Plan ahead and take the pressure off the host.
- NEVER eat anything that you are allergic to just to be polite!
- Picnics and potlucks can be a challenge, so in addition to your potluck food, bring a container of specially prepared food for the allergic person so as to assure that they have a complete meal. Mark the container "Food Allergy" followed by your name. This approach is universally accepted.
- Keep eggless cookies or loaves of eggless quick bread in your freezer—they can be thawed and taken as hostess gifts when you dine at someone else's house, and can also serve as supplemental food for you if part of the meal contains egg.
- Do not offer food to any child without his or her parents' approval. A young child may not fully understand his or her allergies, or may hide the fact that he or she has an allergy because what you are offering looks tasty.
- If your egg-allergic child often visits a certain friend's house, prepare a package of his or her favorite cookies and snacks that can be kept in the freezer at their friend's home, and make sure that the friend's parents or caregivers know of your child's restrictions.
- Keep cupcakes or single portions of eggless cake in the freezer so you are prepared to take a piece of cake to a birthday party at the last minute.
- While a meal is being prepared at a friend's home, visit the kitchen and offer to help. Take an interest in the food and ask about the ingredients—specifically about eggs.
- Remember that even friends who know you well may not totally understand food allergies and all the aspects of living with a food allergy. Nor will they be as knowledgeable about the many foods that contain hidden eggs. You must take the lead.

BE OPEN ABOUT YOUR FOOD ALLERGIES

5. EATING OUT

- Restaurants want healthy customers (who will return!) and are usually willing to work with you; explain your allergy and what you cannot eat. Give your server two choices from the menu that you think might be egg-free, and ask him or her to check with the chef.
- Look up a restaurant's menu online to get an idea of the style of food being served, or call ahead and ask questions.
- Many chain restaurants make food-allergy information available on special menus and online at www .allergysafemenus.com, but still check with your server as a local chef could alter the ingredients.
- Even if a server in a restaurant knows you, restate your food limitations each time you visit.
- Do not be bashful about pleasantly explaining your specific food aller-gies to your waitperson, as well as the seriousness of your request; ask him or her to check with the chef, as ingredients may change from day to day. Most of all, let your server know you appreciate the help.

- If your egg-allergic child is in school, pack a lunch to be safe. Your child may be the envy of his or her table-mates, especially if you occasionally pack an extra cookie or two to share.
- In a college setting, egg-allergic teen-agers should explain their dietary needs to the dorm food manager. If college is away from home, finding a nearby market or health-food store that carries safe products is a must.
- Make a small laminated card for your food-allergic child that explains his or her allergies. If your child is going to eat out with friends, he or she can give it to the host parent or server, who can then accurately educate the chef.
- Before you eat, check your food, as orders may be accidently switched or allergy instructions overlooked. If needed, ask politely to have a new serving prepared and again briefly explain the severity of the allergy.
- If attending a large function, call ahead, ask what is being served, and explain your situation. If the food is being pre-pared off-site or it's a very large event, consider eating before you leave home rather than taking a chance.

DO NOT BE AFRAID TO ASK QUESTIONS AND EXPLAIN YOUR NEEDS

6. TRAVELING AND FOOD ON THE GO

- When traveling by car, bus, or train, plan ahead and be sure to carry some egg-free food with you if your journey stretches over a mealtime. Not all food stops can guarantee safe food.
- Carry your own food on an airplane, as any food served to you is prepared off-site and may not be labeled. An allergic reaction at 25,000 feet is not the easiest to handle, not to mention a sorry way to start a vacation.
- If traveling to a foreign country, contact the country's tourist bureau several weeks before you leave and ask them to translate the following: "I cannot eat eggs in any form or amount, as I have a very serious food allergy to them. Please check with the chef to make sure my meal has not been in contact with egg products. Thank you." Carry extra copies of this translated message with you in case yours does not return from the restaurant kitchen.

TRAVEL EGG-FREE WITH CARE

7. SUGGESTIONS

FOR THOSE NEW TO AN EGG ALLERGY

- If an egg allergy is a new diagnosis, you will find there are many helpful resources, particularly online. See Resources and Information (page 219) for lists of national support groups, egg replacers, foods with hidden eggs, and so on.
- If you're not sure of a food's ingredients, **do not eat it**.
- At home, keep foods that contain eggs properly marked and in a separate cupboard, so a child with allergies will not select the wrong product. Plainly mark any refrigerated or frozen food, such as mayonnaise or cookies made with eggs, with a big red *X* on the lid. (Keep a red Sharpie and some file labels or masking tape in your kitchen drawer for this purpose.)

- If a product lists "natural flavoring," do not assume the product is safe. Contact the manufacturer to find out what the natural flavoring contains.
- Begin a collection of new recipes from magazines, the newspaper, or online sources that are eggless or can easily be adapted by using egg replacers.
- Check with your allergist or local hospital resource center for the latest articles and information on egg allergies.
- Occasionally take extra time at the grocery or health-food store to read labels and find new products without eggs. Keep a list of the products you want to try in the future, and another list of products to avoid.

PLAN AHEAD AND BE INNOVATIVE

8. INTRODUCTION
TO COOKING WITHOUT EGGS

Cooking without eggs is no different than trying any other new recipe. However, a few simple, basic guidelines and ingredients are good to know about:

- PREPARING AHEAD OF TIME: Before starting an eggless recipe, have all the ingredients measured and at room temperature. When using an egg replacer, mix it (usually with water or another liquid) at the last minute, as it does not withstand long holding times—five minutes is about the maximum.
- USING EXTRA FLAVORING: Eggless foods generally need a little extra seasoning or flavoring because they lack the flavor provided by eggs.
- REPLACING ONE EGG PER ONE CUP OF FLOUR: A general rule of thumb for eggless baking is that standard recipes calling for more than one cup of flour for every egg required are good candidates for egg substitutes. If the recipe calls for less than one cup of flour per every egg, it is best to choose another recipe. There are exceptions to these basic proportions, however, such as Crêpes (page 82).
- OVERBEATING EGGLESS BATTERS: For tender cakes and baked goods, stir or beat just enough to combine the ingredients, unless otherwise stated. Overbeating causes an eggless product to become tough and sticky when baked.
- MEASURING DRY INGREDIENTS: All flour and dry ingredients should be spooned into the measuring cup and leveled off, rather than scooped out with the measuring cup; the latter method will compact the flour and throw off the ratio of liquid to dry ingredients. Use a knife or other straight-edged tool to level the top.
- SIFTING FLOUR: All recipes call for unsifted all-purpose flour, unless otherwise stated. It is best to sift all the measured dry ingredients together in a bowl before adding the liquids.
- FILLING PANS: Prepare your baking pans or tins before mixing the batter so that you can immediately fill them once the batter is mixed. Let the filled tins rest at room temperature for a few minutes in order to allow the rising agent to begin working before the heat of the oven creates a crust on the product.
- CHOOSING A PAN SIZE: If the correct-size pan is not available, it's better to bake cakes and breads in

a slightly larger pan rather than a smaller one (eggless batter or dough does not rise well when it is poured in too thick a layer).

- USING ACIDS TO IMPROVE RISING: I have found that recipes with buttermilk, lemon juice, or vinegar (assuming the flavors are appropriate) rise better than those using water or milk to replace the liquid normally found in eggs.
- SLICING BREADS: Eggless breads have a tendency to be a little crumbly, so do not be tempted to slice them when they have just come out of the oven. Let them cool completely and they will slice more easily.
- FREEZING EXTRA PORTIONS: Double recipes when convenient. Use extra-large muffin tins or small casseroles to freeze extra portions. When frozen solid, unmold the containers, wrap the food in plastic, and label each bundle with a name and date. Consider keeping an extra layer of cake and roll of cookie dough in the freezer so you can have dessert in a pinch.
- FLEXIBILITY OF EGGLESS BAKING: Baking without eggs requires flexibility and experimentation because there are so many variables, such as the grind and moisture content of the flour, using margarine vs. butter, knowing the exact temperature of the oven, whether you beat the ingredients by hand or by mixer, and so on.

BE A CREATIVE COOK AND ENJOY

GLOSSARY OF INGREDIENTS

BUTTER, SHORTENING, AND COOKING OIL: Each of these oils has different properties, and in many cases one can be substituted for another. Shortening generally has a low moisture content and may be substituted for butter, cup for cup. However, 7/8 cup of cooking oil equals 1 cup of butter. Butter will give baked goods more flavor than shortening, and cooking oil will not be suitable as a substitute for butter in cakes, as it will not have the light quality of butter when whipped. One more note: whenever butter is called for in this book, it is salted butter.

CAKE FLOUR: This flour is made from low-protein wheat and is usually bleached, which gives it a very fine texture that is preferable for cakes. It takes just 7/8 cup all-purpose flour to substitute for 1 cup cake flour. (Always sift cake flour after measuring.)

CRUMBS: Dried leftover bread or cake may be ground into crumbs and stored in a closed jar in the freezer, to be used for toppings and stuffing.

EGG REPLACER: Egg replacers are powders that, when mixed with water, approximate eggs in recipes. (Note that the proportions of egg replacer to liquid may vary for different recipes and brands.) In some instances, the egg replacer is sifted in with the dry ingredients. In most cases, mix the egg replacer powder with water and let it set for 1 minute to dissolve. Whisk the powder and water until foamy, then add the mixture to the recipe with the other liquids. (Ener-G Egg Replacer has been used for many of the recipes in this book; however, there are several other brands on the market to choose from. Check Resources and Information, page 220, for other options.) Whatever brand you choose, store your egg replacer in a tight-lidded jar in a cool place to preserve its active ingredients.

GELATIN POWDER: Use gelatin to help bind ingredients and add moisture. Add dissolved gelatin powder to meatloaves and meatballs if they are to be served chilled and sliced. I use Knox brand, but there are others on the market.

MARGARINE: Solid margarine in cubes contains 85 percent fat and can be substituted for butter in most recipes; however, avoid diet margarines, as they contain too much water to successfully be used in baked goods.

MAYONNAISE: All references to mayonnaise are for eggless mayonnaise.

MILK: All recipes that call for milk will work with either whole milk or 2 percent milk, unless otherwise specified. Skim milk should not be substituted. Many recipes call for scalding the milk before continuing; just follow the instructions in the recipe.

OIL: Corn, safflower, and canola oils are healthy, neutral-tasting oils that can be used in baked goods. When substituting oil for butter, the baking time may need to be increased 2 to 5 minutes.

OLIVE OIL: The distinctive flavor of olive oil makes it suitable for sautéing and for dressing salads, but it is not recommended for baked goods.

PASTA: Most hard pastas do not contain eggs, but always check the label! As a rule, most fresh pastas do contain eggs.

SELF-RISING FLOUR: All-purpose flour and self-rising flour are not interchangeable—self-rising flour contains leavening and salt. Recipes in this book generally use all-purpose flour.

TOFU: For baked goods and eggless sauces and dressings, silken tofu (the softest kind of tofu) is best to use. Firmer tofu tends to crumble and will not work.

WONDRA FLOUR: Gold Medal is the producer of this low-protein flour that has been treated to be used as an instant thickener for sauces. It has qualities that make it ideal for eggless crêpe batter and will also make pastry flakier. It is available in supermarkets. An acceptable substitute is cake flour that has been sifted at least three times in a flour sifter before measuring.

XANTHAN GUM: The addition of a small amount of xanthan gum gives baked goods a longer shelf life, acts as a thickener, and reduces crumbling. It may appear expensive, but a little goes a long way, and it has a unique ability to enhance eggless products.

Xanthan gum is a polysaccharide (a particular type of molecule) used in many everyday packaged foods and some all-purpose flour blends. To use xanthan gum, add ¼ to ½ teaspoon to 1 cup of flour, and stir it in well. It dissolves when mixed with liquids, and this activates its binding qualities. Xanthan gum may be added to baked goods that contain leavening and ground meat if the product has a tendency to crumb. It is sold in most markets and is typically found in the flour section.

PANTRY STAPLES AND BASIC EQUIPMENT

Eating eggless does not require obscure products or equipment; however, there are a few specialty items that will greatly enhance your eggless baking—powdered egg replacer and xanthan gum chief among them. Other than that, just a few pantry staples are necessary for eggless recipes. You may already have many of these items on hand, and if not, you can find them in most supermarkets and kitchenware stores.

THE BASIC PANTRY:

- Applesauce in individual-size containers (so you can use just what you need for a recipe)
- Baking powder
- Canned evaporated milk
- Cornstarch
- Eggless mayonnaise (usually found chilled in the deli section of stores)
- Egg replacer powder
- Gelatin (unflavored)
- Wondra flour
- Xanthan gum

THE BASIC EQUIPMENT:

There are a few items of cookware that will make eggless cooking easier and more successful; however, specialized equipment is not necessary. In most cases, the following items are meant as suggestions:

- A small wire whisk will easily whip powdered egg replacer into a small quantity of water.
- Several small bowls (½- to ⅔-cup size) are handy for combining egg replacer and water or holding small quantities of ingredients.
- Parchment paper keeps cakes and cookies from sticking to pans and baking sheets, and keeps drop cookies from spreading too much.
- A handheld electric mixer works very well as a substitute for an electric stand mixer.

EQUIPMENT WISH LIST:

- Magic Bullet mixer
- Electric blender
- Food processor, small or standard size
- Ice-cream maker

MUFFINS AND QUICK BREADS

TIPS AND HINTS

- **Handling the Batter:** Mix eggless muffin and bread batters gently and by hand; overworking will cause the product to be tough and sticky.

- **Measuring the Flour:** This step is critical. All recipes in the book call for the flour to be spooned into the measuring cup. Using the cup measure to scoop up the flour directly from its container will compact the flour by a tablespoon or more, and this will make the product too stiff.

- **Zesting Citrus Fruits:** Remove the fragrant, colorful outer layer of oranges and lemons (do not include the white pith) by using the fine holes of a standard cheese grater or a zesting tool such as a Microplane.

- **Pan Size:** If the suggested size is not available, it is better to use a pan for loaf and quick breads that is slightly larger rather than smaller (eggless batter or dough does not rise well when it is poured in too thick a layer).

- **Preparing Baking Tins and Loaf Pans:** All baking tins must be well greased, and loaf pans should be greased and lightly dusted with flour. Teflon muffin tins should be lightly sprayed with cooking oil, as should paper cupcake liners.

- **Filling the Pans:** Do not overfill baking pans, otherwise the dough may spread out over the lip of the pan and look like a large mushroom. Filling pans or tins ⅔ full is a good rule of thumb. Spoon dough into the prepared pan immediately after it is mixed so the rising process will not begin in the mixing bowl.

- **Resting Time Before Baking:** It's important to let eggless muffins rest in the pan for 5 minutes and quick breads for 10 minutes *before* placing them in the oven. This step is very important, as it gives the leavening a chance to begin working before the heat of the oven forms a crust on the food and inhibits rising.

- **Baking Temperature for Muffins:** For best results, bake muffins at 375 to 400 degrees Fahrenheit. The moisture in the dough turns to steam at this temperature and creates lighter muffins. If using a convection oven, lower the temperature setting 10 degrees and reduce the baking time by 2 to 3 minutes.

- **Checking for Doneness:** Insert a toothpick into the center of the baked good. If it comes out clean without crumbs and the bread is pulling away slightly from the sides of the pan, it is done. It is best to not overbake eggless baked goods, as they dry out easily.

- **Cutting and Serving Quick Breads:** Most eggless breads have a tendency to crumble more easily when warm, so avoid the temptation to slice the bread immediately after it is removed from the oven. Breads that are cooled to room temperature and then wrapped in plastic for 4 to 6 hours can be sliced more thinly.

- **Glazing Hard-Crusted Breads and Rolls:** Create an egg wash–type glaze on loaves of bread when they are just out of the oven by brushing them with melted butter.

- **Doubling Muffin or Quick Bread Recipes:** Make a double recipe of dough only if you will be able to bake the whole batch at one time, as the leavening will lose its rising power while waiting for oven space.

- **Making Bread Crumbs:** Dry leftover eggless bread and grind it into crumbs. Keep the crumbs in a tight-lidded jar in the freezer to use for stuffing and toppings.

- **Freezing Muffins and Breads:** Eggless muffins and breads freeze well. To defrost, wrap one or two muffins or a slice or two of bread in a paper towel or napkin and microwave for 12 to 17 seconds on high power. If the breads are sliced before freezing, single slices can be easily brought out to toast.

BLUEBERRY MUFFINS WITH STREUSEL TOPPING

Blueberry muffins are all-time favorites, and the streusel topping, with a hint of lemon, only adds to their appeal.

Makes 12 standard-size muffins

TOPPING

¼ cup firmly packed brown sugar
2½ tablespoons flour
¾ teaspoon grated lemon zest
1 tablespoon butter or margarine, softened

MUFFINS

1½ cups all-purpose flour
¾ cup granulated sugar
2 teaspoons baking powder
1 teaspoon grated lemon zest
¾ teaspoon cinnamon
½ teaspoon salt
4 tablespoons (½ stick) butter or margarine, melted
1¼ teaspoons Ener-G Egg Replacer, whisked with 1½ tablespoons water until foamy
¾ cup milk
1½ cups fresh or frozen blueberries

Preheat the oven to 375 degrees. Grease a standard-size muffin tin.

TOPPING: In a small bowl, stir the sugar, flour, lemon zest, and butter or margarine with a fork until the mixture is crumbly. Set aside.

MUFFINS: In a medium bowl, mix the flour, sugar, baking powder, lemon zest, cinnamon, and salt. In a separate bowl, combine the melted butter or margarine, egg replacer mixture, and milk. Add the liquids all at once to the flour mixture. Stir gently, adding the blueberries last. The batter will be quite stiff, but do not overmix it. Fill the prepared muffin tins two-thirds full and top with the streusel topping. Let the batter rest at room temperature for 5 minutes before placing it in the oven.

Bake for about 20 minutes, or until a toothpick inserted into the center of the muffins comes out clean. Cool the muffins in the tins for 5 minutes before turning out onto a wire rack to cool completely.

LEMON MUFFINS

These tangy, citrusy muffins are delicious served alongside a salad for lunch. If you like lemon-poppy seed muffins, add 2 teaspoons of poppy seeds to the dry ingredients before adding the wet ingredients.

Makes 12 standard-size muffins or 24 mini muffins

MUFFINS

1¾ cups all-purpose flour
¾ cup granulated sugar
1 teaspoon baking powder
¾ teaspoon baking soda
¼ teaspoon salt
1 cup lemon yogurt
4 teaspoons fresh lemon juice
6 tablespoons (¾ stick) butter or margarine, melted and cooled slightly
1 teaspoon Ener-G Egg Replacer, whisked with 2½ tablespoons water until foamy

GLAZE

¼ cup fresh lemon juice
3 tablespoons granulated sugar
1 tablespoon grated lemon zest

Preheat the oven to 400 degrees. Grease a standard-size muffin tin or a mini-muffin tin.

MUFFINS: In a large bowl, sift the flour, sugar, baking powder, baking soda, and salt. In a medium bowl, stir together the yogurt, lemon juice, butter or margarine, and egg replacer mixture. Add the liquids all at once to the flour mixture and stir only enough to dampen the flour. The batter will be a little lumpy, but do not overmix it. Fill the prepared muffin tins two-thirds full. Let the batter rest at room temperature for 5 minutes before placing it in the oven.

Bake standard-size muffins for 18 to 20 minutes; bake mini muffins for 10 to 12 minutes, or until a toothpick inserted into the center of the muffins comes out clean.

GLAZE: While the muffins are baking, make the glaze. In a small saucepan, combine the lemon juice, sugar, and lemon zest. Stir and cook over medium heat until sugar is dissolved, or microwave for 1 minute in a microwave-safe container, then stir until sugar is dissolved.

Remove the muffins from the oven and let rest for 5 minutes. Turn them out onto a wire rack, punch holes in the top of each muffin with a small skewer, and drizzle the hot glaze over them, dividing the glaze evenly between all the muffins. Continue to cool on the rack.

BASIC MUFFINS AND VARIATIONS

Eat these muffins plain, customize them to your liking with the options below, or experiment with some of your favorite ingredients. Club soda, an alternate ingredient for leavening, is used here in place of an egg replacer.

Makes 8 standard-size muffins or 18 mini muffins

1½ cups all-purpose flour
2 tablespoons granulated sugar
1 tablespoon baking powder

½ teaspoon salt

4 tablespoons (½ stick) butter or margarine, melted and cooled to room temperature

¾ cup milk

¼ cup low-fat sour cream

2 tablespoons club soda

Preheat the oven to 375 degrees. Grease a standard-size muffin tin or a mini muffin tin.

In a large bowl, sift the flour, sugar, baking powder, and salt. In a small bowl, mix the butter or margarine, milk, and sour cream with a whisk until smooth. Add the butter mixture and the club soda to the flour mixture and stir with a fork until just combined. Do not overmix the batter. Fill the prepared muffin tins two-thirds full. Let the batter rest at room temperature for 5 minutes before placing it in the oven.

Bake standard-size muffins for 18 to 20 minutes; bake mini muffins 12 minutes, or until a toothpick inserted in the center of a muffin comes out clean. Cool the muffins in the tin for 5 minutes before turning out onto a wire rack.

VARIATIONS

CHEESE-ROSEMARY MUFFINS: Omit the sugar. Add ¾ cup finely grated sharp cheddar cheese and 1 teaspoon crushed dried rosemary to the flour mixture; mix lightly with a fork. Bake for about 20 minutes.

APRICOT MUFFINS: Add 2 tablespoons additional sugar and 3 finely chopped apricots to the dry ingredients, and add ½ teaspoon vanilla extract to the milk before mixing the batter. Bake about 20 minutes.

CARROT MUFFINS: Add ½ teaspoon cinnamon to the dry ingredients, and stir 1 cup shredded carrots and ½ cup raisins into the finished batter. Bake 20 to 22 minutes.

SURPRISE MUFFINS: Fill each muffin tin half full with batter and drop a teaspoon of your favorite jelly, jam, or orange marmalade in the center of the batter. Add the remaining batter to fill each tin two-thirds full. Bake 20 to 22 minutes.

ORANGE MUFFINS: Increase the sugar to ⅓ cup and add 1 teaspoon grated orange zest to the dry ingredients. Substitute ⅔ cup orange juice and ¼ cup milk in place of the milk and sour cream called for in the basic recipe. Bake at 400 degrees for about

18 minutes, or until a toothpick inserted near the center comes out clean. Cool in the muffin tins for 10 minutes before turning out onto a wire rack.

TOP HAT MUFFINS: This is an especially fun recipe for mini muffins. Add ½ teaspoon nutmeg to the flour mixture. For the top hat, mix ½ cup brown sugar, ⅓ cup all-purpose flour, and ½ teaspoon cinnamon with 2 tablespoons melted butter. Combine well, then top each muffin with 1 teaspoon of this mixture before baking. Bake about 12 minutes.

OATMEAL-APPLE MUFFINS

These muffins have a hearty oat flavor, hints of cinnamon and nutmeg, and chunks of fruit. They're a great choice for breakfast.

Makes 12 standard-size muffins

1 cup raisins tossed with 1 tablespoon flour
1 cup finely chopped baking apple
½ cup vegetable oil
¾ cup milk
½ cup all-purpose flour
⅓ cup granulated sugar
2 teaspoons baking powder
2 teaspoons ground cinnamon
1 teaspoon ground nutmeg
½ teaspoon salt
1 teaspoon Ener-G Egg Replacer, whisked with 2 tablespoons water until foamy
1 cup old-fashioned rolled oats

Preheat the oven to 375 degrees. Grease a standard-size muffin tin.

In a large bowl, stir the raisins, apples, oil, and milk together. Sift the flour, sugar, baking powder, cinnamon, nutmeg, and salt together. Add the flour mixture, egg replacer mixture, and oats to the raisin mixture. Stir all together until just mixed, being careful not to overmix.

Fill the prepared muffin tins two-thirds full. Let the batter rest at room temperature for 5 minutes before placing in the oven.

Bake for 15 to 20 minutes, until a toothpick inserted in the center comes out clean. Cool the muffins in the tin for 5 minutes before turning out onto a wire rack.

BRAN MUFFINS

Start the day in a healthy way with these muffins. The raisins add great textural appeal, though you can omit them if you're not a raisin lover.

Makes 12 standard-size muffins

1 cup All-Bran cereal
1 cup buttermilk
1¼ cups all-purpose flour
½ cup firmly packed brown sugar
1 teaspoon baking soda
¼ teaspoon salt
1½ teaspoons Ener-G Egg Replacer, whisked with 2 tablespoons water until foamy
¼ cup vegetable oil
½ cup golden raisins
¼ cup mashed banana or applesauce

Preheat the oven to 400 degrees. Grease a standard-size muffin tin.

In a large bowl, stir the cereal and buttermilk together. Let rest for 5 minutes. In another large bowl, mix the flour, sugar, baking soda, and salt together and set aside.

Add the egg replacer mixture, oil, raisins, and banana or applesauce to the cereal mixture and stir to mix. Add the flour mixture to the wet ingredients and stir until just mixed. Fill the prepared muffin tins three-quarters full. Let rest at room temperature for 5 minutes before placing in the oven.

Bake for 14 to 16 minutes, or until a toothpick inserted in the center comes out clean. Cool for 5 minutes before turning out onto a wire rack.

POPPY SEED MUFFINS

*Using a biscuit mix makes these muffins come together
quickly and easily. They have a light texture and are
wonderful served warm with butter and honey.*

Makes 8 standard-size muffins

1½ cups Bisquick mix
½ cup granulated sugar
1 tablespoon poppy seeds
2 teaspoons grated lemon zest
½ cup sour cream
¼ cup milk
1 teaspoon vanilla extract
3 teaspoons Ener-G Egg Replacer, whisked with ¼ cup water until foamy

Preheat the oven to 375 degrees. Grease a standard-size muffin tin.

In a medium bowl, combine the Bisquick, sugar, poppy seeds, and lemon zest. Whisk
to remove any lumps in the biscuit mix. In a small bowl, combine the sour cream, milk,
vanilla, and egg replacer mixture. Pour the liquids all at once into the dry mixture and
stir until just mixed. Fill the prepared muffin tins two-thirds full. Let the batter rest at
room temperature for 5 minutes before placing in the oven.

Bake for about 12 minutes, or until slightly brown on edges. Cool for 5 minutes before
turning out onto a wire rack.

CREAMED CORN MUFFINS

*The cheddar cheese and creamed corn make these muffins
extra hearty, so they are a good accompaniment to serve with
chili and grilled meats. The green taco sauce adds extra zest.*

Makes 10 to 12 standard-size muffins

2¼ cups Bisquick mix
1 cup shredded cheddar cheese
1 (8.5-ounce) can creamed corn (about 1 cup)
⅓ cup milk
¼ cup green taco sauce
3 tablespoons butter, melted

Preheat the oven to 425 degrees. Grease a standard-size muffin tin.

In a large bowl, combine the biscuit mix and cheese. Use a fork to break up any lumps in the biscuit mix. In a separate bowl, combine the creamed corn, milk, and taco sauce. Add the liquids all at once to the dry mixture and stir with a fork until just combined. Fill the prepared muffin tins two-thirds full. Let the batter rest at room temperature for 5 minutes before placing in the oven.

Bake for 10 minutes, then gently remove the muffins from the oven. Quickly brush the tops with the butter and return to the oven. Continue baking for about 10 to 15 minutes more, or until golden. Cool in the muffin tin for 5 minutes before turning out onto a wire rack.

CORNBREAD

Chili and cornbread are a perfect match on a cold winter day!
Serve warm with jalapeño jelly or honey butter (see recipe below).
Cornbread freezes nicely when well wrapped; simply unwrap and
reheat in a 350-degree oven for a few minutes before serving.

Makes 9 (2½-by-2½-inch) squares

1 cup cornmeal
¾ cup all-purpose flour
3 tablespoons granulated sugar
1½ teaspoons baking powder
½ teaspoon salt
½ teaspoon baking soda
½ teaspoon xanthan gum
1 cup buttermilk

⅓ cup vegetable oil or melted butter

1½ teaspoons Ener-G Egg Replacer, whisked with 2 tablespoons water until foamy

Preheat the oven to 425 degrees. Grease an 8-inch square baking pan.

In a large bowl, combine the cornmeal, flour, sugar, baking powder, salt, baking soda, and xanthan gum. In a medium bowl, combine the buttermilk, oil or butter, and egg replacer mixture, then pour over the dry ingredients. Using a fork, stir until just mixed; some small lumps may still be present. Immediately spoon the batter into the prepared pan and spread evenly. Let rest at room temperature for 5 minutes before placing in the oven.

Bake for 16 to 18 minutes, or until a toothpick inserted in the center comes out clean. Turn out onto a wire rack to cool, then cut into squares.

HONEY BUTTER: Beat ½ cup (1 stick) soft butter or margarine and ½ cup honey together in a small bowl.

VARIATIONS

CORN MUFFINS: Spoon the batter into a greased standard-size muffin tin, filling each muffin to two-thirds full. Let rest at room temperature for 5 minutes before placing in the oven. Bake about 12 minutes, or until golden.

TOASTED CORNBREAD: Split the squares of day-old cornbread horizontally and broil until lightly browned. Serve for breakfast with honey butter or your favorite fruit jam.

CHILI-TOPPED CORNBREAD: Ladle a serving of hot chili over split and toasted cornbread squares, then top with grated sharp cheddar cheese and chopped onions.

CRANBERRY-ORANGE BREAD

This is a moist quick bread that keeps well in the freezer and is my family's favorite for the holidays. It is also wonderful toasted for breakfast.

Makes 2 medium loaves or 4 mini loaves

4 cups all-purpose flour
1¾ cups granulated sugar
1 tablespoon baking powder
2½ teaspoons Ener-G Egg Replacer
1 teaspoon baking soda
1 teaspoon salt
2 tablespoons grated orange zest (from 1 large orange)
½ cup (1 stick) cold butter or margarine, cut into cubes
2 cups whole cranberries (fresh or, if frozen, partially thawed), chopped very coarsely
    or cut in half with scissors
1 cup golden raisins
1¾ cups orange juice

Preheat the oven to 350 degrees. Grease and lightly flour two 8-by-4-inch loaf pans or four 4½-by-2½-inch mini loaf pans.

In a large bowl, combine the flour, sugar, baking powder, egg replacer, baking soda, and salt. Stir in the orange zest. Using two knives or a pastry blender, cut the butter or margarine into the flour mixture until it is the size of coarse crumbs. Stir in the cranberries and raisins. Add the orange juice and stir until barely mixed. The batter will be quite stiff; do not overmix. Spoon the batter into the prepared pans. Let the filled pans rest at room temperature for 10 minutes before placing in the oven.

Bake the medium loaves for about 1 hour; bake the mini loaves about 45 minutes, or until a toothpick comes out clean when inserted in the center. Cool the pans on a wire rack for about 10 minutes, then turn out to completely cool before slicing.

VARIATION

APRICOT-RAISIN BREAD: Substitute 2 cups coarsely chopped dried apricots for the cranberries, reduce the sugar to 1¼ cups, and add ¼ cup milk in place of the orange juice.

———————

BANANA BREAD

Serve this bread with morning coffee, or slice and toast it for a midday treat. Golden raisins add moisture and complement the banana flavor.

Makes 1 large loaf

1 cup whole wheat flour
½ cup all-purpose flour
½ cup granulated sugar
½ cup firmly packed brown sugar
1 teaspoon baking soda
½ teaspoon ground ginger (optional)
½ teaspoon salt
⅓ cup (5⅓ tablespoons) butter, melted and slightly cooled, or ⅓ cup vegetable oil
1¼ cups mashed, well-ripened bananas (about 3 small)
½ teaspoon grated lemon zest
¼ cup plain yogurt
1½ teaspoons Ener-G Egg Replacer, whisked with 2 tablespoons water until foamy
⅓ cup golden raisins (optional)

Preheat the oven to 350 degrees. Grease and flour a 9-by-5-inch loaf pan.

In a large bowl, sift together the whole wheat flour, all-purpose flour, sugars, baking soda, ginger, and salt. In a medium bowl, combine the butter or oil, bananas, lemon zest, yogurt, and egg replacer mixture. Stir in the raisins. Fold the banana mixture into the dry ingredients. Stir gently, and do not overmix. Pour into the prepared loaf pan. Let rest at room temperature for 10 minutes before placing in the oven.

Bake for 45 to 50 minutes, or until the bread comes away from the sides of the pan a little. Cool on a wire rack for about 10 minutes, then turn the loaf out onto the rack to cool completely before slicing.

COOK'S NOTE

- If the mashed bananas do not equal 1¼ cup, applesauce may be added to fill the required amount.

ZUCCHINI BREAD

*Make this bread in the late summer or early fall,
when garden-fresh zucchini are so plentiful.*

Makes 1 medium loaf

1 cup coarsely shredded zucchini
1 cup all-purpose flour
1 teaspoon cinnamon
½ teaspoon nutmeg
¼ teaspoon ground ginger
½ teaspoon salt
¼ teaspoon baking soda
¼ teaspoon baking powder
⅔ cup firmly packed brown sugar
⅓ cup vegetable oil
¾ teaspoon vanilla extract
½ teaspoon grated orange zest
1½ teaspoons Ener-G Egg Replacer, whisked with 2 tablespoons water until foamy

Preheat the oven to 350 degrees. Grease and lightly flour an 8-by-4-inch loaf pan.

Press the grated zucchini between layers of paper towel to squeeze out as much liquid as you can. Set aside.

Sift the flour, cinnamon, nutmeg, ginger, salt, baking soda, and baking powder together. In a large bowl, beat the sugar, oil, vanilla, and orange zest until blended. Add the zucchini and egg replacer mixture to the sugar mixture and stir well, separating any clumps of zucchini. Gently fold in the flour mixture until just combined. The batter will be stiff. Spoon it into the prepared loaf pan and let rest at room temperature for 10 minutes before placing in the oven.

Bake for about 1 hour and 15 minutes, or until a toothpick comes out clean when inserted into the center of the loaf. Cool on a wire rack for about 10 minutes before turning out onto the rack. Cool completely before slicing.

BEER-BATTER CHEESE BREAD

This savory quick bread goes well with chili or soup and is a wonderful addition to a Monday night football supper. Use a mild American beer, such as Budweiser; dark beer makes the bread bitter.

Makes 1 large loaf

1 (12-ounce) bottle light-bodied beer
3 cups all-purpose flour
3 tablespoons granulated sugar
4 teaspoons baking powder
1 teaspoon salt
3 cups (about 6 ounces) shredded cheddar cheese
½ cup grated Parmesan cheese
½ teaspoon dried oregano (optional)
½ teaspoon dried thyme (optional)
2 tablespoons butter, melted

An hour or so before you make the recipe, pour the beer into an uncovered bowl (to allow it to go flat and come to room temperature) before adding it to the batter.

Preheat the oven to 375 degrees. Grease and lightly flour a 9-by-5-inch loaf pan.

In a large bowl, combine the flour, sugar, baking powder, and salt. Add the cheeses, oregano, and thyme to the flour mixture and stir with a fork to combine. Add the beer and mix well. Spoon the batter into the prepared loaf pan and spread evenly. Pour the melted butter evenly over the top of the batter and immediately place it in the oven.

Bake for 45 to 50 minutes, or until a toothpick inserted into the center of the loaf comes out clean. Cool on a wire rack for about 10 minutes in the pan before turning out onto the rack. Cool completely before slicing.

COOK'S NOTE

- This bread is not a long keeper, so freeze it after 2 days. After thawing, slice and toast the bread, then serve it hot with butter.

BREAKFAST SCONES

Good morning! Enjoy a hot cup of coffee, the morning paper, and a classic breakfast scone. Spread the scone with jam for an extra-special treat.

Makes 6 scones

2 cups all-purpose flour
3 tablespoons granulated sugar, plus 2 teaspoons for topping scones
1 tablespoon baking powder
½ teaspoon salt
1 teaspoon finely grated lemon zest
½ cup (1 stick) cold butter, cut into 8 pieces
⅔ cup milk
½ cup dried currants

Preheat the oven to 400 degrees. Grease a baking sheet or line it with parchment paper.

In a large bowl, combine the flour, 3 tablespoons sugar, baking powder, and salt. Add the lemon zest. Using two knives or a pastry blender, cut the butter into the flour mixture until it is the size of coarse crumbs. Stir in the milk and currants with a fork until the dough is evenly moistened; do not overwork the dough. With floured hands, gather the dough into a ball and knead four to five times. Form the dough into a disk about 8 inches across and 1 inch thick.

Place onto the prepared baking sheet. Using a floured knife, cut through the dough to make 6 wedges, but do not separate the pieces. Sprinkle the dough with the remaining 2 teaspoons of sugar.

Bake for 15 to 18 minutes, or until the scones are a light brown. Recut the scones into wedges and serve warm.

ORANGE ZEST SCONES

*The infusion of orange zest and yogurt makes these scones
moist and tender with just the right amount of orange flavor.
Enjoy them fresh out of the oven at breakfast time.*

Makes 6 scones

2 cups all-purpose flour
4 teaspoons baking powder
¼ teaspoon baking soda
¼ teaspoon salt
2 teaspoons grated orange zest
4 tablespoons (½ stick) cold butter, cut into 4 pieces
¾ cup orange-flavored yogurt (from one 6-ounce carton)
¼ cup orange juice
1 tablespoon granulated sugar, for topping scones

Preheat the oven to 400 degrees. Grease a baking sheet or line it with parchment paper.

In the bowl of a food processor, combine the flour, baking powder, baking soda, salt, and orange zest. Pulse twice to combine. Add the butter and pulse until crumbly. In a small bowl, stir the yogurt and orange juice together and pour them evenly over the flour mixture. Pulse a few times until barely mixed.

With floured hands, gather the dough together and form it into a disk about 8 inches across and 1 inch thick. Place onto the prepared baking sheet. Using a floured knife, cut the disk into six wedges, but do not separate the pieces. Sprinkle the dough with the sugar.

Bake for 15 to 18 minutes, or until the scones are a light brown. Recut the scones into wedges and serve warm.

COOK'S NOTE

- To mix by hand, use a medium bowl and cut in the butter with two knives or a pastry blender. Stir in the liquids and continue as above.

BUTTERMILK BISCUITS

Consider making a double batch of these buttery, slightly tangy biscuits; any leftovers are wonderful split, toasted, and topped with honey or jam for breakfast. Or split and spread them with Dijon mustard, then fill them with ham and cheese to accompany a bowl of soup. Yet a third option is to add 1 tablespoon of sugar to the dough and serve with sugared strawberries for a summer shortcake.

Makes 8 to 12 biscuits

2 cups all-purpose flour
1 teaspoon salt
1 tablespoon baking powder
½ teaspoon baking soda
4 tablespoons (½ stick) cold butter or shortening, cut into cubes
¾ cup buttermilk

Preheat the oven to 425 degrees. Grease a baking sheet or line it with parchment paper.

In a large bowl, combine the flour, salt, baking powder, and baking soda. Cut the butter or shortening into the flour mixture with a pastry blender or two knives until it resembles large crumbs. Gently stir in the buttermilk with a fork until the dough forms a large, loose ball.

Place the dough on a floured surface and knead it five times. Pat the dough out to about ½-inch thickness and cut into 8 to 12 biscuits with a floured round cookie cutter.

Place the biscuits on the prepared baking sheet and bake for 8 to 10 minutes, until they are lightly brown on top.

VARIATIONS

DESSERT BISCUITS: Add ¼ cup sugar to the flour mixture. Sprinkle extra sugar on top of each biscuit before baking.

BUTTERMILK DROP BISCUITS: Increase the buttermilk to 1 cup. Do not overmix. Drop by large spoonsful onto a prepared baking sheet and bake for 9 to 12 minutes. If using for the top of a cobbler or a meat pie, place the casserole in the oven and bring the contents up to temperature before dropping the biscuits on top.

BREAKFAST AND BRUNCH

TIPS AND HINTS

BREAKFAST OPTIONS

Since eggs figure prominently in breakfast menus, this meal is where creativity
comes into play for eggless eaters. Just
remember that breakfast does not have to
mean traditional egg dishes. Many muffin,
pancake, and waffle recipes can be made
eggless. With a few additions, a bowl of
oatmeal can easily be taken beyond a
breakfast basic. Leftover rice with milk
and sugar makes a great simple breakfast.
If there are foods you particularly enjoy at
other meals, why not try chicken noodle
soup, leftover quiche, crispy chicken, or a
slice of meatloaf for breakfast?

TIPS FOR PANCAKES AND WAFFLES

- **Stirring the Batter:** Be sure to stir the
  batter only until most of the lumps
  have disappeared (some small lumps
  are okay); overbeating will make pancakes or waffles tough.

- **Batter Consistency:** The batter for
  eggless pancakes and waffles always
  needs to be just a little thicker than
  standard egg batter (to make up
  for the thickening power of eggs).
  Because of this, it is easier to ladle

the batter onto the griddle than to
pour it. If necessary, spread the batter
immediately after it is ladled onto the
pancake griddle or the waffle iron.

- **Griddle Temperature for Pancakes:**
  For larger and thicker pancakes, lower
  the heat a little so they will cook all
  the way through before becoming too
  brown.

- **Making Waffles:** Eggless waffles
  require a little patience. Be sure to
  spray the waffle iron with nonstick
  cooking spray before each batch. Do
  not open the waffle iron during the
  first few minutes of baking, as this
  will cause the waffle to split in half.
  Wait until steam stops escaping; you
  should find that the lid lifts easily at
  that point.

- **Waffle-Iron Temperature:** The temperature of waffle irons varies, and
  this affects the amount of liquid to be
  used in the batter, so make a test waffle and adjust the liquid in your recipe. If the waffle batter is too thin and
  the temperature of the iron is not high
  enough, the excess liquid will steam
  and cause the waffles to be limp, not
  crispy.

- **Freezing:** Extra cooked pancakes and waffles are always handy to have in the freezer. Waffles reheat quickly in the toaster, and pancakes are simple to warm up in a lightly greased sauté pan.

- **Egg Alert:** There are a number of egg-free pancake and waffle mixes on the market now, but still be sure to read the list of ingredients carefully every time you make a purchase, as the manufacturers may add or remove ingredients, and this information can vary even by package size.

BREAKFAST BISCUIT SANDWICH

Biscuit sandwiches are perfect for a brunch buffet, as biscuits freeze well and can be reheated before filling. Loosely cover the thawed biscuits with a sheet of aluminum foil and heat them in a 350-degree oven until warmed, then assemble the sandwiches for your guests. If you're also cooking for those who can eat eggs, a fried egg would make this an extra-hearty breakfast.

Makes 10 biscuits

2 cups all-purpose flour
1 teaspoon salt
2¼ teaspoons baking powder
½ teaspoon baking soda
½ cup (1 stick) cold butter, cut into 8 pieces
¾ cup low-fat buttermilk
½ cup strawberry jam
8 ounces country ham
5 ounces cheddar cheese, sliced

Preheat the oven to 375 degrees. Grease a baking sheet or line it with parchment paper.

In a medium bowl, combine the flour, salt, baking powder, and baking soda. Using two knives or a pastry blender, cut the butter into the flour mixture until it resembles coarse crumbs. Add the buttermilk and stir it in with a fork to form a rough dough. Flour your hands and knead the dough in the bowl five or six times to combine all the loose bits; transfer to a floured surface.

Pat the dough out to about ¾-inch thickness and cut into 3½-inch biscuits using a floured round cookie cutter. Collect the scraps and reshape them to make additional biscuits so that you have 10 biscuits (put the scraps inside the cookie cutter and mold them to fit). Place the biscuits onto the prepared baking sheet.

Bake for about 15 minutes, until lightly browned. Transfer to a wire rack.

To finish the sandwiches, cool the biscuits slightly, split them in half, and spread a generous amount of jam on the top half of each biscuit. Place ham and cheese slices on the bottom halves, then cover with the biscuit tops. Serve warm.

HAM BENEDICT

This makes a festive brunch dish when accompanied by a bowl of fresh fruit. You'll never even miss the eggs.

Serves 4

12 ounces sliced Canadian bacon
4 English muffins
2 large tomatoes
1 (10-ounce) package frozen chopped spinach, thawed
Salt and freshly ground pepper
½ cup grated cheddar cheese, or 8 slices American cheese
1 ripe avocado, peeled and cut into 8 wedges

HOLLANDAISE SAUCE

1 (0.9-ounce) packet Knorr Hollandaise Sauce Mix
½ teaspoon dry mustard
¾ cup plus 2 tablespoons milk
4 tablespoons (½ stick) butter
1 tablespoon fresh lemon juice
Dash Tabasco sauce

Preheat the oven to 325 degrees.

In a skillet, sauté the Canadian bacon lightly until warmed but not browned. Drain on a paper towel. Split the muffins and toast them lightly.

Slice off the stem end from each tomato and cut each into 4 thick slices. Place the slices on a paper towel to absorb excess juice. Cook the spinach as directed on the package.

Spread it out to drain; when cool enough to handle, squeeze out all excess moisture, and season with salt and pepper.

HOLLANDAISE SAUCE: In a small saucepan, combine the sauce mix, mustard, and milk. Cook over medium heat, stirring with a whisk until well blended and beginning to thicken. Add the butter and bring to a simmer, then continue to simmer for 1 to 2 minutes, stirring frequently until thickened and smooth. Remove from the heat and stir in the lemon juice and Tabasco sauce.

Place the toasted muffin halves on a baking sheet, cut side up, and top each with Canadian bacon, a thin layer of cooked spinach, then a slice of tomato. Bake for 8 minutes, just until the tomatoes are heated through. Top each half with 1 tablespoon grated cheese and bake for 2 more minutes, or until the cheese is melted.

Immediately place two muffin halves on each plate. Drizzle with hot hollandaise sauce, and top with an avocado wedge. Place the remaining sauce in a small bowl to pass at the table.

COOK'S NOTE

- To keep the sauce warm for up to 1 hour, place the covered saucepan in a larger pan of simmering water, stirring occasionally. The sauce may also be covered and chilled for a few hours, then reheated in the microwave using one-third power.

APPLE AND SAUSAGE BURRITOS

Kids and adults alike love these burritos—they are a great breakfast on the go. Plus, they're easy to make, freeze well, and reheat quickly. For a more leisurely, decadent knife-and-fork breakfast, top them with maple syrup.

Makes 8 burritos

4 cooking apples, peeled, cored, and thinly sliced
1 tablespoon butter
2 tablespoons granulated sugar
¼ cup firmly packed brown sugar
2 tablespoons fresh lemon juice
1 tablespoon cinnamon
2 pounds bulk sausage meat or links
8 (10-inch) thin flour tortillas

Preheat the oven to 350 degrees. Grease a 13-by-9-inch baking dish.

In a skillet, sauté the apple slices in the butter for 10 minutes, or until soft and beginning to brown. Remove the pan from the heat and add the sugars, lemon juice, and cinnamon. Stir to blend well; set aside.

In a separate sauté pan, crumble the sausage meat and cook until lightly browned, breaking up any clumps of meat. When thoroughly cooked, transfer it to a plate lined with a paper towel. Discard the fat.

Divide the apples and sausage among the eight tortillas, placing the filling on one half. Roll up and place in the baking pan, seam side down. Bake uncovered for 12 to 15 minutes for crisp tortillas. If you want the tortillas to be soft, cover the pan loosely with foil and bake for about 25 minutes.

VARIATION

Make a double batch of Crêpes (page 82) and use in place of the tortillas for a special brunch. Place ¼ cup of the apple-sausage filling on each crêpe. Fold the three sides of the crêpe in as you roll them up, then follow the burrito recipe above. Dust the tops lightly with a mixture of cinnamon and sugar after baking. Serve topped with warm maple syrup or whipped topping. Makes 12 crêpes.

COOK'S NOTES

- These can be made up to 12 hours ahead. Cover the unbaked burritos and refrigerate them. Bring them to room temperature, then cover the pan loosely with foil and bake for 20 to 25 minutes, or until heated through.

- The filled burritos can also be frozen for later use. To cook individual frozen burritos, put them on a microwave-safe plate and cover them with a paper towel. Microwave until heated through. Watch out for the hot filling!

HONEY-VANILLA GRANOLA WITH DRIED FRUIT

The dried fruit gives this granola great texture and flavor. It's also nut-free, though you can add ½ cup of your favorite chopped nuts for even more crunch.

Makes 2¼ quarts

4 cups old-fashioned rolled oats
½ cup firmly packed brown sugar
¼ cup oat bran (optional)
3 tablespoons vegetable oil
2 tablespoons honey
1½ teaspoons vanilla extract
¼ teaspoon salt
½ cup chopped dried apples, dried apricots, or mixed dried fruits
¼ cup dried cranberries
¼ cup golden raisins
1 tablespoon finely chopped crystallized ginger

Preheat the oven to 300 degrees.

Place the oats, sugar, and bran onto an ungreased 10-by-15-inch baking sheet that has sides about 1 inch high. Mix well. In a saucepan, combine the oil, honey, vanilla, and salt and bring to a simmer. Pour the oil mixture over the oat mixture and toss to combine. Distribute the mixture evenly in the baking sheet and bake for 10 minutes. Remove from the oven and toss again.

Add the dried fruits and ginger, then toss to distribute the fruit. Again spread evenly over the baking sheet and bake for 10 to 15 minutes more, or until the oats are crisp.

Remove from the oven and toss several times while the mixture is cooling. When completely cool, store the granola in an airtight container for up to 2 weeks, or freeze for up to 1 month.

FRUITED OATMEAL

*Chock-full of fruit, this oatmeal is rich in vitamins
as well as being very flavorful and filling.*

Makes 2 generous servings

¾ cup milk
1 cup water
¾ cup old-fashioned rolled oats
¼ teaspoon salt
¼ cup diced dried apple
¼ cup dried cranberries
¼ cup golden raisins
½ banana, sliced
Brown sugar, for topping
Plain yogurt, for topping

In a medium saucepan, bring the milk and water just to a boil. Lower the heat and add the oats and salt. Stir to combine and simmer, uncovered, for 2 minutes, stirring occasionally.

Add the apple, cranberries, and raisins, and simmer for 1 minute more. Cover the pan and remove it from the heat. Let stand for 2 to 3 minutes.

Spoon the oatmeal into bowls and top with some of the sliced banana, sugar, and yogurt.

BUTTERMILK PANCAKES WITH BLUEBERRIES

These pancakes have been a Sunday morning family favorite for years! The batter can also be adapted for waffles (see Variations that follow).

Makes 16 medium pancakes

2 cups all-purpose flour
2 tablespoons granulated sugar
1 teaspoon baking powder
¾ teaspoon baking soda
½ teaspoon grated lemon zest (optional)
¼ teaspoon nutmeg
½ teaspoon salt
2 cups buttermilk
3 tablespoons vegetable oil
1 tablespoon Ener-G Egg Replacer, whisked with 3 tablespoons water until foamy
1 cup blueberries, fresh or frozen and thawed
Pancake syrup or whipped honey

Heat a griddle or large pan over medium heat.

In a medium bowl, combine the flour, sugar, baking powder, baking soda, lemon zest, nutmeg, and salt. Add the buttermilk, oil, and egg replacer mixture to the flour mixture. Stir until barely blended, then add the blueberries. Stir again. Let the batter rest for 5 minutes.

Grease the griddle and spoon ¼-cup portions of batter onto the preheated griddle. Slightly spread the pancake batter with the back of the spoon. Cook until bubbles just begin to form on the surface. Flip each pancake and cook until the underside is golden brown. Serve with butter and syrup or your topping of choice.

VARIATIONS

BUTTERMILK WAFFLES: Omit the blueberries and add ¼ cup low-fat sour cream with the liquids in the recipe. Lightly spray the waffle iron with cooking spray just before adding the batter.

BELGIAN WAFFLES: Place a generous spoonful of sweetened whipped cream over each buttermilk waffle and top with sugared, sliced strawberries and a dusting of confectioners' sugar.

CREAMY RICOTTA TOPPING FOR PANCAKES AND WAFFLES

This delicious topping is heavenly on pancakes and waffles. With a dash of freshly grated nutmeg, it's also wonderful on fresh fruit. The topping needs to be made ahead of time to give the flavors time to meld; put it together the night before and it'll be one less thing you have to do in the morning!

Makes 2½ cups

2 cups low-fat cottage cheese
½ cup low-fat ricotta cheese
1 tablespoon brown sugar
2 teaspoons fresh lemon juice
Dash of freshly grated nutmeg

Line a sieve with a paper coffee filter or paper towel. Suspend the sieve over a bowl and add the cheeses. Stir, cover with plastic wrap, and set in the refrigerator for 1 to 2 hours, letting the excess liquid drain from the cheeses.

Discard the liquid. Place the cheese mixture in a food processor and add the sugar, lemon juice, and nutmeg. Blend until smooth. Place the mixture in a serving bowl and cover with plastic wrap. Refrigerate at least 6 hours before serving.

FRIED POLENTA

*While the rest of the family was having French toast, my mother
would make these browned cornmeal cakes for me. I called them
"fried mush" and would top them liberally with maple syrup
before inhaling them. Using a store-bought roll of precooked
polenta (available in markets, usually near the dried pasta)
makes for simple and speedy cooking, although you may use
homemade polenta if you have it (see Cook's Notes below).*

Serves 4

1 (18-ounce) roll polenta
All-purpose flour, for dusting
1 tablespoon vegetable oil
1 tablespoon butter
Pancake syrup or whipped honey

Cut the polenta into ½-inch-thick slices and pat them dry with a paper towel. Dust
lightly with flour. Heat the oil and butter in a sauté pan over medium heat. Lay the
sliced polenta in the pan, but do not overlap the pieces. Brown each side until crisp and
golden. Repeat if necessary until all the polenta has been browned. Serve topped with
warm pancake syrup or whipped honey.

COOK'S NOTES

• Any leftover, unbrowned polenta may be repurposed for dinner. Slice and place
it in a greased baking pan. Heat it in a hot oven until lightly browned and serve it
topped with marinara sauce—or brush the tops of the slices with olive oil, top with
pesto sauce, and bake in a 450-degree oven for 10 to 12 minutes until the edges are
a little crisp.

• Pour your home-cooked polenta into a pan and spread it to ¾-inch thickness.
Refrigerate. When cold and set up, cut with a round cookie cutter or slice it into
squares. Cook as above.

FRENCH TOAST

*For a special breakfast, pair this eggless French toast
with strips of crispy bacon and a bowl of fresh fruit.*

Makes 6 slices

6 slices firm whole wheat bread
1 cup evaporated canned milk (undiluted)
1 tablespoon granulated sugar
1 teaspoon Ener-G Egg Replacer
½ teaspoon cinnamon
¼ teaspoon nutmeg
¼ teaspoon salt
1 teaspoon vegetable oil
Pancake syrup, or other toppings of your choice

Place the bread on a wire rack and cover with a paper towel. Let it air dry for 1 hour or
more; this will allow the bread to absorb more liquid.

Whisk the milk, sugar, egg replacer, cinnamon, nutmeg, salt, and oil in a small bowl.
Arrange the bread slices so they are touching but not overlapping in a flat pan with
sides, then pour the milk mixture evenly over the slices. Let rest for 1 minute, then
turn the slices using a fork and spatula to prevent tearing. Cover and refrigerate for 15
minutes so more liquid is absorbed.

Spray a large, nonstick sauté pan or flat griddle with cooking oil and preheat it over
medium-high heat. Using a slotted spatula and fork, transfer the bread slices to the pan
or griddle and cook until brown on both sides. Adjust the temperature as needed so
the toast is cooked through but not overly browned. Respray the pan between batches.

Serve with pancake syrup.

SAUSAGE AND MUSHROOM BRUNCH CASSEROLE

*This casserole combines the savory flavors of sausage, mushrooms,
and meat in a rich cheese sauce. It is wonderful for a winter
brunch buffet and can be prepared the day before, refrigerated,
and baked just before serving. Freeze individual portions of
leftovers and reheat them for a quick, hearty breakfast.*

Serves 10

6 tablespoons (¾ stick) butter
6 tablespoons all-purpose flour
4 cups milk
2 tablespoons white wine
¼ cup minced fresh parsley
¼ teaspoon dried thyme
¼ teaspoon salt
¼ teaspoon freshly ground pepper
¼ teaspoon Worcestershire sauce
1 cup fresh bread crumbs
½ cup grated cheddar cheese
1½ pounds link or bulk sausage
½ pound button mushrooms, sliced
2 cups precooked chopped ham, shredded turkey, or chicken
½ pound sharp cheddar cheese, cut into ⅓-inch cubes

Preheat the oven to 350 degrees. Grease a 9-by-13-inch casserole dish.

In a medium saucepan, cook the butter and flour together until bubbling. Slowly whisk in the milk and continue cooking and stirring until the sauce begins to bubble again and thicken. Add the wine, parsley, thyme, salt, pepper, and Worcestershire sauce. Stir and remove from the heat. Set aside.

Place the bread crumbs in a pie pan and toast in the oven for 5 minutes, or until just barely brown. Cool the crumbs and combine with the grated cheese; set aside.

Break up the sausage meat (if using links, cut them into bite-size pieces) and place in a sauté pan. Cook until browned, breaking up any large clumps of meat. Transfer the sausage to a plate lined with a paper towel. Discard all but 1 tablespoon of the fat from the sausage and use that to sauté the mushrooms. Add the mushrooms and cook over medium-high heat until their moisture has evaporated and they are slightly browned.

Evenly distribute the sausage; ham, turkey, or chicken; mushrooms; and cubed cheese in the prepared casserole dish. Cover with the sauce and sprinkle the cheese and bread crumbs mixture over the top. Bake for 40 to 45 minutes, or until heated through and crisp on the top.

COOK'S NOTE

- The casserole may be covered and refrigerated overnight before baking. Bring it to room temperature before placing it in the preheated oven.

BREAKFAST CHIMICHANGAS WITH FRESH FRUIT

Rich with ricotta and cream cheese, studded with strawberries, and bursting with aromatic notes of lemon, vanilla, and cinnamon, these sweet chimichangas are always a showstopper at brunch. They also serve as a marvelous dessert.

Serves 6

8 ounces (1 cup) cream cheese, softened
⅓ cup ricotta cheese
¼ cup plus 1 tablespoon granulated sugar
1 teaspoon grated lemon zest
1 teaspoon vanilla extract
¾ teaspoon cinnamon
¾ cup sliced strawberries, plus more for garnish
6 (7-inch) flour tortillas
2 teaspoons butter

2 teaspoons vegetable oil
½ cup sour cream
¼ cup strawberry preserves

Beat the cream cheese, ricotta, sugar, lemon zest, vanilla, and cinnamon in a medium bowl. Add the strawberries to the cheese mixture and fold in to blend. Place one-sixth of the cheese-strawberry mixture in the center of each tortilla. Fold two sides in and fold the opposite side over to enclose filling and form a square.

In a medium nonstick skillet, heat the butter and oil over medium heat. When hot, place the tortillas seam side down in the pan. Cook for 1 to 2 minutes until lightly golden brown, then turn and continue to brown them for 1 to 2 minutes more. Place on a paper towel to absorb the oil and serve hot, topped with a spoonful of sour cream and a small spoonful of strawberry preserves.

BANANA SMOOTHIE

*The lemon juice adds a nice tartness to this
combination of otherwise sweet fruits.*

Makes 1 serving

½ banana, cut into 1-inch pieces
½ cup orange juice
4 strawberries, hulled
1 tablespoon fresh lemon juice
¼ cup plain nonfat yogurt
1 teaspoon honey

Combine all the ingredients in a blender and blend until smooth. Pour into a chilled glass and serve.

TOMATO-CUCUMBER SMOOTHIE

*Almost like a Bloody Mary! Add vodka
and you have the real drink.*

Makes 1 serving

2 medium-size ripe tomatoes, or 1 cup cherry tomatoes
½ medium English cucumber, peeled
½ bell pepper, seeded
Dash of Worcestershire sauce
Pinch of salt
Dash of Tabasco sauce

Coarsely chop the tomatoes, cucumber, and bell pepper. Process the tomatoes, cucumber, pepper, Worcestershire sauce, salt, and Tabasco sauce in the blender until smooth. If desired, strain to remove any seeds. Serve in a chilled glass.

SOUTH SEAS SMOOTHIE

*The smooth texture and mellow flavors of tropical
fruits make for a classically delicious smoothie. It takes
you back to that Hawaiian vacation you took.*

Makes 1 serving

⅔ cup chopped fresh mango
⅔ cup chopped pineapple (fresh or canned)
½ banana, cut into 1-inch pieces
¼ cup vanilla low-fat yogurt

Combine the mango, pineapple, and banana in a blender and blend until smooth. Add the yogurt and blend until just combined. Serve in a chilled glass.

SALADS AND SALAD DRESSINGS

TIPS AND HINTS

- **Using Eggless Mayonnaise**: A number of the salad dressings in this chapter use store-bought eggless mayonnaise to give the dressing a creamy quality and thicker texture. It is also the base for a few sauces. To make your own mayonnaise, see Homemade Eggless Mayonnaise (page 74), where you'll also find many tasty variations on mayonnaise dressings.

- **Blending Oils for Dressing**: Remember that oils that are stored in the refrigerator, like nut oils, may need some time at room temperature to warm back to a liquid state in order for the ingredients to blend well.

- **Freshness of Oils**: Smell or taste the oils you plan to use for salad dressings to ensure they are fresh-tasting; nothing can ruin a salad faster than "off" or rancid oil. Before purchasing olive and specialty oils, check their color, clarity, and pull dates.

- **Lemon Juice**: I prefer using salad dressings made with lemon juice rather than vinegar when I'm serving wine with a meal. The flavors complement each other nicely.

- **Onions for Salad**: Soak sliced or chopped raw onions for 30 minutes in a bowl of ice water with a pinch of salt, then drain them well and dry. This will tame their pungent flavor and make them milder and more palatable.

GREEN PEA SALAD WITH HORSERADISH CREAM DRESSING

This unusual salad is a buffet favorite: the green apple adds crunch, the bacon lends a nice savoriness, and the dressing has a tangy zip to it. The recipe is from California Heritage Continues, *and I thank the Junior League of Pasadena, California, for permission to use it here. If you have any leftover dressing, it's nice on steamed vegetables or as a sandwich spread.*

Serves 4 to 6

DRESSING

½ cup low-fat sour cream
2 teaspoons prepared horseradish
2 teaspoons fresh lemon juice
½ teaspoon salt
⅛ teaspoon freshly ground pepper

SALAD

1 (10-ounce) package frozen green peas or petits pois
1 tart Granny Smith apple, unpeeled, cored, and coarsely chopped
3 green onions, thinly sliced (including green portion)
4 to 5 slices bacon
Lettuce leaves, for serving

DRESSING: Combine the sour cream, horseradish, lemon juice, salt, and pepper in a small bowl. Stir together well, cover, and chill for one hour.

SALAD: Place the peas in a colander and rinse under hot, running water until just thawed. Drain thoroughly. Combine the peas, apple, and green onions in a large bowl.

Toss with enough horseradish dressing to coat. Cover and refrigerate for several hours or overnight.

Cut the bacon into ½-inch pieces and fry until crisp. Drain on a plate lined with paper towels. (The bacon may be cooked ahead and refrigerated or frozen, then rewarmed before serving.)

Just before serving, add the crisp bacon to the salad and toss. Add additional dressing to taste. Spoon the salad onto a serving platter or bowl lined with lettuce leaves.

OLD-FASHIONED POTATO SALAD

Potato salad and picnics are a classic combination. Both the dressing and the potatoes may be prepared the day before and refrigerated separately, and then mixed together several hours before serving to allow the flavors to meld.

Serves 8 to 10

DRESSING

1 cup eggless mayonnaise
¼ cup low-fat sour cream or yogurt
2 teaspoons Dijon mustard
1 teaspoon French's yellow mustard (optional—it adds nice color)
2 tablespoons fresh lemon juice
2 teaspoons celery seed (optional)
1 teaspoon granulated sugar
½ teaspoon salt
Pinch of freshly ground pepper

SALAD

2 pounds large waxy potatoes, unpeeled
1 teaspoon salt
2 tablespoons cider vinegar
2 tablespoons chicken broth (or reserve 2 tablespoons water after cooking the
    potatoes)
⅓ cup minced yellow onion
1 cup finely chopped celery
3 tablespoons chopped fresh parsley
3 tablespoons finely chopped sweet pickle
3 tablespoons finely chopped green onion (including green portion)
Salt and freshly ground pepper
Lettuce leaves, for serving
Chopped parsley, for garnish

DRESSING: In a small bowl, whisk the mayonnaise, sour cream or yogurt, mustards, lemon juice, celery seed, sugar, salt, and pepper until well combined. Cover and chill for 1 hour to blend the flavors.

SALAD: Place the potatoes in a large pot and cover with cold water. Add the salt and bring the water to a boil. Lower the heat and simmer until the potatoes are tender when pierced with a fork; if you overcook them, the potatoes will crumble when combined with the dressing. Drain the potatoes, reserving some water if desired, and when they are cool enough to handle, peel and cut them into ½-inch chunks.

Place the warm potatoes into a large bowl and pour the cider vinegar and chicken broth or reserved potato water over them. Toss gently with a rubber spatula. Let the potatoes absorb the liquid for 15 minutes.

When the potatoes are completely cooled, add the onion, celery, parsley, pickle, and green onions. Season to taste with salt and pepper. Fold in ¾ cup of the mayonnaise dressing, saving the last ¼ cup to add at serving time if the potatoes seem dry. Cover and chill for several hours. Remove the salad from the refrigerator 30 minutes before serving, taste for seasoning, and toss gently.

Serve in a bowl lined with lettuce leaves and garnish with chopped parsley.

FRENCH POTATO SALAD

This is a light, mayo-free potato salad with an herbed oil-and-vinegar dressing. It pairs beautifully with grilled meats and especially with Italian sausage at a summer barbecue—and because it does not contain dairy products, this salad travels well to a picnic.

Serves 6

2 pounds small red or other waxy potatoes, unpeeled
¼ cup fresh lemon juice
1 teaspoon Dijon mustard
3 cloves garlic, minced
1 teaspoon dry mustard
½ teaspoon salt
¼ teaspoon freshly ground pepper
⅓ cup olive oil
⅓ cup finely chopped red onion
2 tablespoons chopped fresh parsley
1 tablespoon minced fresh oregano, or ½ teaspoon dried oregano
Lettuce leaves, for serving

Steam the potatoes until just tender when pierced with a fork. Drain the potatoes and set aside. When cool enough to handle, peel and cut them into bite-size pieces.

While the potatoes are cooking, whisk the lemon juice, Dijon mustard, garlic, dry mustard, salt, and pepper in a small bowl. Add the olive oil in a slow stream and whisk until the dressing starts to thicken.

Add the red onion, parsley, and oregano to the potatoes and toss with enough dressing to coat lightly. Cover and chill for several hours to combine the flavors. At serving time, add additional dressing, if desired, then toss gently and spoon the salad into a lettuce-lined serving bowl.

FAR EAST POTATO SALAD

*This piquant, Asian-inspired potato salad goes well with
teriyaki chicken and a side of steamed vegetables.*

Serves 4

1 pound waxy potatoes, unpeeled
½ cup chopped celery
½ cup sliced water chestnuts
⅓ cup eggless mayonnaise
2 teaspoons wasabi (Japanese horseradish)
1 tablespoon fresh lime or lemon juice
¼ teaspoon salt

Steam the potatoes until just tender when pierced with a fork. Drain the potatoes and set aside. When cool enough to handle, peel and cut them into cubes.

In a medium bowl, combine the potato cubes, celery, and water chestnuts. In a small bowl, whisk together the mayonnaise, wasabi, lime or lemon juice, and salt. Add the dressing to the potato mixture and toss the salad gently with a rubber spatula.

Cover and chill for several hours before serving. At serving time, toss the salad gently to redistribute the dressing.

CAESAR SALAD

*This light version of the classic Caesar dressing contains
no egg—perfect for those who have allergies or who simply
prefer to avoid eating raw eggs. The original Caesar
salad is said to have been created in 1924 by Caesar
Cardini at his restaurant in Tijuana, Mexico.*

Serves 8

CROUTONS

2 cloves garlic, minced
3 tablespoons olive oil
1 French baguette, cut diagonally into 8 (½-inch-thick) slices

DRESSING

¼ cup fresh lemon juice
2 large cloves garlic, minced or pressed
1 tablespoon eggless mayonnaise
1½ teaspoons anchovy paste, or 2 finely minced anchovy fillets
¼ teaspoon salt
1 teaspoon Worcestershire sauce
½ teaspoon freshly ground pepper
½ cup canola oil
½ cup olive oil

SALAD

3½ quarts romaine lettuce (about 2 heads), cut into bite-size pieces
½ cup freshly grated Parmesan cheese

CROUTONS: Combine the garlic and olive oil and let stand for 30 minutes. Preheat the oven to 325 degrees. Brush the oil mixture onto one side of each baguette slice and place on a baking sheet. Bake until very lightly toasted, about 10 to 12 minutes. Set aside.

DRESSING: In a small bowl, whisk together the lemon juice, garlic, mayonnaise, anchovy paste or fillets, salt, Worcestershire sauce, and pepper until well blended. Start adding the canola oil very slowly while whisking the dressing. If oil collects on the top of the dressing, stop adding oil and whisk until it is emulsified. Continue whisking while slowly adding the olive oil until the dressing is slightly thickened.

Place the romaine in a large serving bowl. Pour sufficient dressing over the greens to moisten. Toss and add more dressing if desired. Add the Parmesan and toss again. Check the seasoning and adjust with more salt, pepper, or lemon juice. Garnish each serving with a crouton.

VARIATION

CHICKEN CAESAR: Preheat the oven to 375 degrees. Dip 2 boneless, skinless chicken breast halves in a light oil-and-vinegar salad dressing and shake off the excess. Coat chicken with ⅓ cup grated Parmesan cheese and place on a greased baking sheet. Bake for 20 minutes, or until the meat is no longer pink in the center but is still moist. Transfer it to a plate and slice across the grain into ½-inch pieces; place the slices on top of the dressed salad. If you want to bake the chicken ahead of time, wrap and chill it for 1 day, then bring it to room temperature before slicing and serving.

CREAMY COLESLAW

The early Dutch settlers who came to the Lower Hudson Valley in the 1600s created recipes for coleslaw, as cabbage was plentiful and it stored well. This coleslaw has a little tang and is nice with corned beef. Make it a few hours ahead of time so the flavors can blend.

Serves 6

½ cup low-fat sour cream
½ cup eggless mayonnaise
2 teaspoons Dijon mustard
1½ tablespoons granulated sugar
4 teaspoons white wine vinegar
1 teaspoon celery or caraway seeds
½ teaspoon salt
Pinch of freshly ground pepper
8 cups shredded green cabbage (from a 1-pound package or a 1¾-pound head)
1 Granny Smith apple, unpeeled, cored, and coarsely chopped

In a small bowl, combine the sour cream, mayonnaise, mustard, sugar, vinegar, celery or caraway seeds, salt, and pepper. Stir until well mixed.

In a large bowl, combine the cabbage and apples. Toss with enough dressing to moisten, but do not overdress. The salad will become moister and the flavors will blend nicely if chilled for several hours before serving.

THE WEDGE WITH BLUE CHEESE DRESSING

The retro wedge salad has returned, with all the trimmings but without that pesky egg.

Serves 4 to 6

DRESSING

½ cup eggless mayonnaise
¼ cup red wine vinegar
1 tablespoon olive oil
1½ teaspoons granulated sugar
1 clove garlic, finely minced
¼ teaspoon Dijon mustard
¼ teaspoon salt
¼ teaspoon freshly ground pepper
4 ounces blue cheese, crumbled (about 1 cup), or more to taste
¼ cup low-fat sour cream
½ cup buttermilk

SALAD

1 head iceberg lettuce, well chilled
1 avocado, cut into cubes
2 medium tomatoes, seeded and chopped (about ¾ cup)
2½ ounces blue cheese, crumbled (about ⅔ cup)
¾ pound bacon, cooked and crumbled (about 1 cup)

DRESSING: Place the mayonnaise, vinegar, oil, sugar, garlic, mustard, salt, and pepper into the bowl of a blender or food processor and pulse for 10 seconds until well blended. Add the blue cheese, sour cream, and buttermilk. Pulse until just blended (you want some lumps to remain). Pour the dressing into a bowl, cover, and chill until ready to serve.

SALAD: Remove any wilted outside leaves from the head of lettuce. Strike the bottom of the head on a flat surface to loosen the core. Pull or cut out the core and cut the head into 4 or 6 wedges, depending on how many people you are serving. Place each wedge on its side on a salad plate. Sprinkle the avocado, tomatoes, blue cheese, and bacon (in that order) evenly over each lettuce wedge.

Drizzle 2 tablespoons of dressing over each wedge. Pass the remaining dressing at the table.

MACARONI SALAD

Who doesn't love pasta salad? This version is extremely versatile—you can vary the ingredients to suit your palate. I often substitute chopped cooked shrimp or cubes of cheese for the ham. It's a good choice for potluck gatherings, and can be made the day before.

Serves 4 to 6

DRESSING

½ cup eggless mayonnaise
2 tablespoons sour cream
1 tablespoon fresh lemon juice
1 teaspoon Dijon mustard
2 tablespoons chopped dill pickle
2 tablespoons chopped red bell pepper
1 tablespoon finely chopped olives (black or green)
2 green onions, thinly sliced (including green portion)
1 tablespoon chopped fresh parsley

SALAD

1¾ cups (6 ounces) uncooked elbow macaroni
1 tablespoon vegetable oil
½ cup finely diced ham

½ cup chopped celery
Dash of freshly ground pepper

DRESSING: In a small bowl, combine the mayonnaise, sour cream, lemon juice, and mustard and whisk until well blended. Add the pickle, red pepper, olives, green onions, and parsley and mix well. Cover and chill if not using immediately.

SALAD: Boil the macaroni in salted water according to the package directions. Drain and place the macaroni in a large bowl. Drizzle with the oil and toss to coat the pasta. Cool to room temperature, tossing occasionally.

Spoon three-quarters of the dressing over the cooled macaroni. Add the ham, celery, and pepper and fold in until well mixed. Cover and chill for at least 1 hour before serving to blend flavors.

At serving time, add additional dressing if desired. Toss and serve.

ORCHARD SALAD WITH GINGER DRESSING

This refreshing salad is a wonderful addition to a summer buffet and travels well to a potluck. Our farmers' markets abound with many varieties of berries, melons, and tree fruits that can be enjoyed plain or prepared for salads like this one.

Serves 8

DRESSING

¾ cup low-fat sour cream
2 tablespoons orange marmalade
2 tablespoons minced crystalized ginger
½ teaspoon Dijon mustard

SALAD

Select from the following choices—you will need about 8 cups of assorted fresh fruit.

Grapefruit sections
Orange sections
Cantaloupe balls
Watermelon cubes
Pineapple tidbits
Green grapes
Papaya wedges
Mango chunks
Kiwi slices
Blueberries
Raspberries
Strawberries, cut in half if large

DRESSING: Combine the sour cream, marmalade, ginger, and mustard in a small bowl and stir well to blend. Cover and chill for several hours to blend the flavors before serving.

SALAD: Prepare the fresh fruit and combine it in a serving bowl, or display it separately on a platter lined with lettuce leaves. Pass the dressing for spooning onto individual servings of fruit.

PIQUANT CHICKEN SALAD

The addition of chunks of crisp apple gives this chicken salad a refreshing, tart bite. For an attractive presentation, line the plate with a lettuce leaf, and then mound the salad on top of crescent-shaped slices of cantaloupe.

Serves 6

DRESSING

½ cup eggless mayonnaise

2 tablespoons vegetable oil
4 teaspoons fresh lemon juice
2 teaspoons minced fresh ginger
1 teaspoon soy sauce
1 teaspoon Dijon mustard
1 clove garlic, smashed and minced
½ teaspoon granulated sugar
½ teaspoon salt
Dash of freshly ground pepper

SALAD

4 cups shredded or cubed cooked chicken breast
½ Granny Smith apple, unpeeled, cored, and chopped into ⅓-inch pieces
1 cup chopped celery
1 tablespoon minced green onion (including green portion)
Lettuce leaves, for serving
Cantaloupe wedges, for serving
½ cup slivered almonds or minced parsley, for garnish (optional)

DRESSING: In a small bowl, mix the mayonnaise, oil, lemon juice, ginger, soy sauce, mustard, garlic, sugar, salt, and pepper.

SALAD: In a large bowl, combine the chicken, apple, celery, and onions. Stir to mix, then add enough dressing to moisten the ingredients. Cover and chill for 1 hour. Spoon the salad onto plates lined with lettuce leaves and cantaloupe slices. Garnish with the almonds or parsley.

VARIATION

For a more classic chicken salad, omit the apple and increase the celery to 1½ cups. Also omit the ginger and soy sauce in the dressing.

CURRIED CHICKEN SALAD

The curry and lemon add a Middle Eastern flavor to this chicken salad. For a special luncheon, serve the salad atop a ring of pineapple on dinner plates lined with lettuce, with toasted pita bread on the side. If you don't have (or don't like) water chestnuts, increase the celery to 2 cups.

Serves 8 as a main course

DRESSING

½ cup eggless mayonnaise
½ cup low-fat yogurt
⅓ cup mango chutney, chopped if very chunky
2½ teaspoons curry powder
1 teaspoon grated lemon zest
¼ cup fresh lemon juice
2 teaspoons soy sauce
⅛ teaspoon paprika

SALAD

4 cups shredded cooked chicken or turkey breast
1 cup chopped celery
1 (6-ounce) can water chestnuts, drained and chopped
1½ cups red grapes, cut in half
½ cup minced green onions (including green portion)
½ cup chopped peanuts or currants, for garnish (optional)

DRESSING: In a small bowl, combine the mayonnaise, yogurt, chutney, curry powder, lemon zest and juice, soy sauce, and paprika; whip together with a fork. Cover and refrigerate.

SALAD: In a large bowl, combine the chicken or turkey, celery, water chestnuts, grapes, and green onions. Toss with the dressing, cover, and refrigerate for several hours to combine the flavors before serving.

Garnish with the peanuts or currants.

VARIATION

PITA BREAD SANDWICH: Cut 4 pieces of whole-wheat pita bread in half crosswise, opening each to make a pocket. Spread each pocket with eggless mayonnaise, dividing ½ cup mayo between the 8 halves. Shred 4 cups of lettuce and place ½ cup in each pita half. Spoon ⅓ cup chicken salad on the lettuce and garnish with halved red grapes or chopped peanuts. For smaller sandwiches, cut each filled half sandwich in half again, garnish, and stand with triangle points up in a narrow serving dish.

PASTA COBB SALAD

This salad is a variation on the traditional Cobb salad, with extra chicken and cheese replacing the traditional chopped boiled eggs. It can be a side dish or can stand alone as a complete meal.

Serves 8 as a main course

DRESSING

¼ cup white wine vinegar
1 tablespoon minced fresh parsley
2 teaspoons Dijon mustard
2 teaspoons fresh lemon juice
½ teaspoon freshly ground pepper
1½ teaspoons honey
2 cloves garlic, minced
1 teaspoon Worcestershire sauce
⅔ cup olive oil

SALAD

1 pound dried pasta (small shells or fusilli)
2 cups shredded cooked chicken meat
12 ounces bacon, fried and crumbled (optional)
¾ cup pitted black olives, quartered
½ cup crumbled blue cheese (about 2 ounces)
3 to 4 medium tomatoes, seeded and chopped
2½ cups firmly packed fresh spinach leaves
1 avocado, cubed

DRESSING: Combine the vinegar, parsley, mustard, lemon juice, pepper, honey, garlic, and Worcestershire sauce in a jar with a screw lid. Shake well to mix. Add the oil, cover the jar tightly with the lid, and shake well. Refrigerate for at least 1 hour so the flavors have time to blend.

SALAD: Cook the pasta according to the package directions until al dente and drain it well. Place the hot pasta in a large bowl and add half the dressing. Stir until all the pasta is coated. Cool to room temperature, stirring several times to allow all the pasta to absorb the dressing. Add the chicken, bacon, olives, cheese, and tomatoes to the pasta. Toss to coat all the ingredients with the dressing. Cover and chill until serving time (at least 1 hour or up to 1 day).

Just before serving, cut the spinach crosswise into strips. Add it, along with the avocado, to the salad. Drizzle in a bit more dressing if needed, then give everything a final, gentle toss. Serve any remaining dressing in a separate bowl.

ORZO AND SHRIMP SALAD

The ingredient list for this salad may look long, but trust me: the recipe is simple, and the dish comes together quickly. If you don't eat seafood, use sliced grilled chicken in place of the shrimp. Feta cheese crumbles and chopped red pepper are also nice additions.

Serves 6

1 teaspoon salt
½ pound orzo pasta
2 tablespoons olive oil
Dash of freshly ground pepper

DRESSING

1 clove garlic, minced
1 tablespoon Dijon mustard
2 tablespoons fresh lemon juice
2 tablespoons olive oil
⅓ cup eggless mayonnaise
¼ cup sour cream or yogurt
2 to 3 teaspoons chopped fresh dill, or ¾ teaspoon dried dill
Salt and freshly ground pepper

SALAD

¾ pound medium raw shrimp in the shell, or ½ pound precooked, shelled shrimp
1 to 2 medium tomatoes, seeded and coarsely chopped
¼ cup Kalamata olives
⅓ cup minced fresh parsley
4 fresh basil leaves, chopped, or ½ teaspoon dried basil
3 green onions, thinly sliced (including green portion)
1 avocado, cubed

Add the salt to 3 quarts (12 cups) of water in a large pot. Bring the water to a boil. Add the orzo and cook for about 8 minutes, or until just tender. Drain well and turn into a large bowl. While the pasta is still warm, drizzle it with the olive oil and add the black pepper. Toss to combine; cool the orzo to room temperature. Proceed to the next step, or cover and refrigerate the pasta overnight.

DRESSING: While the pasta boils, combine the garlic, mustard, lemon juice, olive oil, mayonnaise, sour cream or yogurt, dill, salt, and pepper in a small bowl. (The dressing can also be made the day before and refrigerated, covered.)

SALAD: If using raw shrimp: Prepare a 4-quart pot of boiling salted water and carefully add the shrimp. When the water returns to a boil, lower the heat and simmer for about 3 minutes (depending on the size of the shrimp), until the shrimp turn pink and are slightly firm. Immediately drain and run cool water over them. Peel and devein the shrimp, place them in a small bowl, and toss with 2 tablespoons of the dressing. Cover and chill.

If using precooked shrimp: While the pasta is cooking, place the shrimp in a small bowl and drizzle with 2 tablespoons of the dressing. Toss, cover, and chill.

An hour before serving, toss the chilled orzo, shrimp, tomatoes, olives, parsley, basil, green onions, and additional dressing together. Check the seasoning and return to the refrigerator to blend flavors. Just before serving, add the avocado and toss again.

SEAFOOD LOUIS

All the ingredients for this throwback classic of seafood in an (eggless) Thousand Island dressing may be prepared ahead, covered, and chilled separately, making the preparation easy when it's time to eat. Serve with crusty French bread on the side.

Makes 4 main-course servings

DRESSING

1 cup eggless mayonnaise
½ cup low-fat sour cream
¾ cup Heinz chili sauce or ketchup
1 tablespoon fresh lemon juice
2 teaspoons prepared horseradish
2 teaspoons minced yellow onion
2 tablespoons finely chopped dill pickle
¼ teaspoon Worcestershire sauce

SALAD

1 cup fresh cooked crabmeat

1½ cups cooked, peeled, and deveined medium-size shrimp
1½ cups chopped celery
½ cup green onions, thinly sliced (including green portion)
1 medium head iceberg lettuce, or 1 large head leaf lettuce
2 medium tomatoes, cut into small wedges

DRESSING: In a small bowl, combine the mayonnaise, sour cream, chili sauce or ketchup, lemon juice, horseradish, onion, pickle, and Worcestershire sauce. Whisk together until well blended. Cover and chill for 1 hour.

SALAD: In a large bowl, combine the crab, shrimp, celery, and green onions. Add half the dressing to the seafood, toss gently, cover, and chill for 1 hour before serving.

Place one large leaf of lettuce on each salad plate, or, if serving family style, place several leaves in a wide, shallow serving bowl. Shred the remaining lettuce and divide it between the individual salad plates (or add it to the wide, shallow bowl). Spoon the seafood salad over the shredded lettuce and garnish with tomato wedges. Pass any remaining dressing at the table in a separate bowl.

GREEN GODDESS DRESSING

The creaminess of this dressing goes wonderfully with the crunch of romaine lettuce. It also makes a festive dip for boiled, chilled, and peeled shrimp (reduce the sour cream to ¼ cup if serving as a dip).

Makes 1 cup

½ cup eggless mayonnaise
2 tablespoons minced green onions (including green portions)
1 teaspoon chopped fresh tarragon
1 tablespoon minced fresh parsley
1 tablespoon fresh lemon juice
1 clove garlic, minced
1½ teaspoons anchovy paste
¼ teaspoon salt
¼ teaspoon freshly ground pepper
⅓ cup low-fat sour cream

In the bowl of a blender or small food processor, combine the mayonnaise, green onions, tarragon, parsley, lemon juice, garlic, anchovy paste, salt, and pepper. Blend until smooth. Scrape the sides of the blender. Add the sour cream and pulse until just blended.

Spoon the dressing into a small bowl, then cover and refrigerate for 1 hour to blend the flavors before serving. Tightly covered, this dressing will keep for up to 2 days in the refrigerator.

CLASSIC VINAIGRETTE

Oil-based dressings are lighter than mayonnaise-based dressings (even eggless ones). This is a traditional vinaigrette, but feel free to experiment with different oils and flavored vinegars that suit your taste or complement your salad ingredients. When dressing delicate greens, I prefer to substitute lemon juice for vinegar—its flavor is less assertive.

Makes 1⅓ cups

1 clove garlic, minced
½ teaspoon salt
¾ teaspoon Dijon mustard
⅛ teaspoon freshly ground pepper
⅓ cup white wine vinegar or fresh lemon juice
1 cup canola oil or light olive oil

In a small bowl, mash the garlic and salt with the back of a teaspoon until a rough paste forms. Add the mustard and pepper, stirring until well mixed. Whisk in the vinegar or lemon juice.

Add the oil very slowly while continually whisking. If oil collects on the top of the dressing, stop adding it and whisk vigorously until the dressing emulsifies. Continue until all the oil has been added.

This dressing may be stored in a tightly-covered jar in the refrigerator for up to 2 weeks. Bring it to room temperature, then whisk with a fork until the dressing is well mixed.

VARIATION

HERB VINAIGRETTE. Just before serving, stir in 1 tablespoon minced parsley or 1 teaspoon of minced fresh, fragrant herbs such as tarragon, oregano, dill, basil, or thyme.

COOK'S NOTE

- For a thicker and creamier dressing, use an electric hand mixer, blender, or immersion blender to combine as above. For a speedy dressing (although less creamy), make the garlic/salt paste, then put it into a large jar with a lid. Add the rest of the ingredients, put the lid on, and shake until well mixed.

TOFU MAYONNAISE

Extra seasonings such as fresh lemon juice, Tabasco sauce, and dry mustard give this light, eggless mayonnaise a tangy, zesty taste that works well on sliced tomatoes or poached vegetables.

Makes 1 cup

6 ounces silken tofu
2 teaspoons Dijon mustard
1 tablespoon white wine vinegar
½ teaspoon salt
Dash of Tabasco sauce
2 tablespoons fresh lemon juice
¼ teaspoon dry mustard
2 tablespoons light olive or canola oil

In the bowl of a blender or small food processor, combine the tofu, Dijon mustard, vinegar, salt, Tabasco sauce, lemon juice, and dry mustard. Pulse 10 times. Add the oil 1 tablespoon at a time and process until well blended and smooth.

Transfer the mayonnaise to a jar with a tight-fitting lid and refrigerate for at least 1 hour. The mayonnaise may be stored for up to 5 days in the refrigerator.

HOMEMADE EGGLESS MAYONNAISE

The shelf life of homemade mayonnaise is short—just 5 days—but it's worth the effort for a special salad. Make sure your oil is fresh tasting and at room temperature before making the mayonnaise. (If it's too cold, it won't blend well.) If you'd like to make a nondairy version of this mayonnaise, you may substitute silken tofu for the sour cream.

Makes 2 cups

2 tablespoons sour cream
1 tablespoon fresh lemon juice
½ teaspoon dry mustard
½ teaspoon salt
Pinch of white pepper
1 cup vegetable oil, at room temperature
1 cup light olive oil, at room temperature

In the bowl of a blender or a medium-size food processor, combine the sour cream, lemon juice, mustard, salt, and pepper; blend until smooth. Next, open the small hole in the lid of the blender or food processor, and with the motor running, very slowly begin drizzling in the vegetable oil. Once it has emulsified, add the olive oil in the same way.

You may also make the mayonnaise by hand by whisking the sour cream, lemon juice, mustard, salt, and pepper in a medium bowl until smooth. Next, slowly drizzle in the vegetable oil while continuing to whisk quickly. Be sure the oil is emulsifying and not separating from the other ingredients. Add the olive oil in the same manner.

When all the oil has been added and the mayonnaise has thickened, taste and correct the seasoning. Store the mayonnaise in a container with a tight lid. Refrigerate for up to 5 days.

VARIATIONS

Add any of the following to 1 cup of eggless mayonnaise and whisk to combine. Cover and chill for 1 hour to blend the flavors.

HERB-GARLIC MAYONNAISE: Add ½ teaspoon sugar, 1 small clove crushed garlic, ½ teaspoon chopped chives, ¼ teaspoon dried basil, ½ teaspoon dried oregano, ¼ teaspoon salt, and ½ cup low-fat yogurt. Blend well and serve as a sandwich spread.

CREAMY MAYONNAISE: Add ½ cup low-fat ricotta cheese, ½ teaspoon Dijon mustard, 1 tablespoon fresh lemon juice, and a dash of cayenne pepper. Blend well and serve on sliced tomatoes.

GREEN MAYONNAISE: Add 3 finely chopped anchovies, 1½ tablespoons minced parsley, 2 teaspoons minced chives, 1 teaspoon drained, minced capers, and a pinch each of dried dill and thyme. Blend well and serve with shellfish or cold beef.

DIJON MAYONNAISE: Add 2 teaspoons Dijon mustard and 1 teaspoon horseradish. Blend well and serve with ham.

RÉMOULADE: Add 1 teaspoon Dijon mustard, ½ teaspoon anchovy paste, 2 teaspoons chopped sweet pickle, 2 teaspoons drained, chopped capers, and 1 tablespoon chopped parsley. Combine well and serve with grilled beef.

PESTO MAYONNAISE: Add 2 tablespoons prepared pesto. Blend well and serve with sliced tomatoes.

WASABI AND LIME MAYONNAISE: Combine 1 teaspoon wasabi paste, 1 teaspoon grated lime zest, and a dash of soy sauce. Stir into mayonnaise and serve with Asian-flavored meats.

COGNAC SAUCE: Add 1½ teaspoons tomato puree and 1½ teaspoons cognac. Stir well and serve with seafood.

MANGO CHUTNEY SAUCE: Add 2 tablespoons chopped mango chutney. Blend and serve with cold, sliced lamb.

HORSERADISH AND APPLE SAUCE: Add 1 tablespoon prepared horseradish and 2 tablespoons minced apple. Blend and serve with corned beef.

CAPER AND PARSLEY SAUCE: Add 1 tablespoon drained, chopped capers, 2 tablespoons minced parsley, and 1 teaspoon fresh lemon juice. Blend and serve with cold roast beef or chicken.

SMALL PLATES, SANDWICHES, AND SAUCES

TIPS AND HINTS

- **Planning Ahead:** Most of these small-plate dishes and sauces can be prepared ahead of time, making the preparation of the rest of the meal faster and easier.

- **Cooking with Children:** Children love to be in the kitchen, and small plates, which are typically less complicated than main courses, are a great opportunity for them to learn basic kitchen skills, as well as about how to prepare eggless foods.

- **Covering a Sauce:** When using plastic wrap to cover a sauce that is to be refrigerated, make sure the wrap is in direct contact with the top of the sauce; this will prevent the sauce from discoloring or forming a film on its surface.

CHEESE AND BACON QUICHE

Quiche, originally from France, became popular in the United States in the 1950s and 1960s, and a cheese and bacon version (originally called quiche Lorraine) was a favorite of many. As pie shells vary in size and depth, it's difficult to be exact about the amount of filling, but if you have any leftover filling, simply bake it in a separate greased baking dish.

Serves 6

1 unbaked 9-inch pie shell
4 ounces (about 5 strips) bacon, diced
1 cup thinly sliced yellow onion
2 tablespoons olive oil
2 cloves garlic, minced
¾ pound peeled zucchini, cut in half lengthwise and then sliced thinly
2 cups firmly packed spinach, finely chopped
1¼ cups seeded chopped tomatoes
2 tablespoons chopped fresh basil
1 tablespoon minced green onion (green part only)
1 teaspoon dried thyme
1 teaspoon grated lemon zest
¼ teaspoon salt
¼ teaspoon freshly ground pepper
¾ cup low-fat ricotta cheese
¼ cup feta cheese
1¼ cup shredded Swiss cheese or farmer's cheese

Have all the ingredients prepared (sliced, minced, chopped, etc.) before starting to cook the filling.

Preheat the oven to 375 degrees. If your piecrust is frozen, set it on the counter to thaw. If you've made a fresh crust, hold it in the refrigerator until assembling the quiche.

Cook the bacon in a large skillet over medium heat until almost crisp. Remove the bacon and set aside on a paper towel to drain. Discard the fat and wipe out the pan with a paper towel. Sauté the onion in olive oil for 3 minutes, then add the garlic and zucchini. Sauté for 12 to 15 minutes, or until the zucchini is soft but not brown. Add the spinach and tomatoes and sauté a few minutes more until the spinach is wilted. Add the basil, green onion, thyme, lemon zest, salt, and pepper; stir to combine. Remove from the heat.

Place the ricotta and feta in a medium bowl and beat with a handheld electric mixer or in a small blender until well combined. Sprinkle the shredded cheese over the vegetables in the sauté pan and add the ricotta mixture. Stir until all ingredients are mixed; spoon the filling into the unbaked pie shell.

Bake for about 40 minutes, or until the filling is set. Cool for 10 minutes, cut into wedges, and serve.

VARIATIONS: Any of these ingredients can be added or swapped for others: 1 cup thinly sliced brown mushrooms, sautéed; ⅓ cup finely chopped red bell pepper; or ¼ cup minced ham.

CRAB CAKES

These are a Pacific Northwest specialty and a real treat.
This recipe has many ingredients, but preparation is easy.
Keep in mind that the cakes need to be chilled for several
hours before browning; otherwise they may break apart.

Serves 6 to 8 as an appetizer

¼ cup finely minced white onion
¼ cup finely minced celery
1 tablespoon vegetable oil
⅓ cup eggless mayonnaise
3 tablespoons fresh lemon juice
2 teaspoons coarse-grained or Dijon mustard
1 teaspoon Worcestershire sauce
1 teaspoon prepared horseradish

1 tablespoon minced parsley
½ teaspoon xanthan gum
1½ teaspoons Ener-G Egg Replacer, whisked with 2 tablespoons water until foamy
¼ teaspoon Tabasco sauce
¼ teaspoon salt
¼ teaspoon freshly ground pepper
½ cup fresh bread crumbs or panko
1 pound fresh cooked crabmeat, shredded with a fork
1 cup panko or other fine dried bread crumbs, for coating cakes
2 tablespoons olive oil
2 tablespoons butter
Tartar sauce, for serving

In a small skillet, sauté the onions and celery in the vegetable oil until soft but not browned. Set aside to cool to room temperature. In a medium bowl, combine the onion-celery mixture, mayonnaise, lemon juice, mustard, Worcestershire, horseradish, parsley, xanthan gum, egg replacer mixture, Tabasco, salt, and pepper. Fold in the ½ cup fresh bread crumbs or panko. Add the crab and stir with a fork until well mixed.

With dampened hands, divide the mixture into 16 patties. Flatten them slightly and coat with panko or bread crumbs. Place in a single layer on a plate, cover, and refrigerate for 1 to 2 hours.

In a large skillet, melt the olive oil and butter over medium-high heat. When the foam subsides, add the crab patties and brown on one side, about five minutes. Turn carefully, using a spatula and a fork (the cakes are fragile); brown on the other side. Serve immediately with Tartar Sauce (page 97) on the side.

COOK'S NOTE

- If fresh crab is not readily available in your area, or if it's too expensive, lightly poached boneless white fish or shredded large shrimp can replace half or all of the crabmeat. I do not recommend canned crab; I don't like its flavor.

EGG ALERT: Be sure to use real crab; artificial crab or crab-flavored seafood products most often contain egg white.

CRÊPES

My daughter, Linda, created the original eggless crêpe recipe, which I have adapted slightly. These thin French pancakes are lovely and can be filled with savory or sweet fillings. A savory recipe follows this one, and sweet recipes are on pages 166–167. Make a double batch; the leftovers freeze beautifully (thaw them for 2 hours at room temperature). Be sure to follow the directions exactly as written to get the right texture.

Makes 6 crêpes

2 tablespoons Ener-G Egg Replacer
2 tablespoons plus ⅓ cup water, divided, at room temperature
1 cup Wondra flour (see Cook's Note)
½ cup whole milk
2 tablespoons vegetable oil
¼ teaspoon salt

In a medium bowl, whisk the egg replacer for a full 2 minutes with the 2 tablespoons water until it is the consistency of lightly whipped egg whites. Let the mixture rest for 10 minutes.

Add the Wondra flour, milk, the remaining ⅓ cup of water, oil, and salt to the egg replacer mixture. Whisk for 30 seconds. Cover the bowl tightly and refrigerate for at least 1 hour but for no longer than 4 hours. The batter should be about as thick as heavy cream. If it is too thin, add 1 teaspoon of Wondra; if it's too thick, add 1 teaspoon of water.

Preheat a nonstick crêpe pan or an 8-inch nonstick sauté pan over medium-high heat; the pan is at the right heat when a few drops of water dropped on the pan's surface bounce. When ready to make the first crêpe, stir the batter gently to incorporate any ingredients that have settled on the bottom of the bowl.

Spray the surface of the pan lightly with cooking oil, or grease the pan with a thin film of butter. Using a ⅓-cup measure, scoop up about ¼ cup of batter. Holding the crêpe pan in one hand and tilting the pan a little, start pouring the batter in a circle around the outer sides of the heated pan, starting at the top side of the pan. When all the batter has been poured around the pan, immediately move it slowly in a circular direction to allow the batter to cover the center of the pan to form the thin crêpe. The crêpe will be slightly thinner in the middle. (Note that this is different from making egg crêpes, where batter is poured into the middle of the pan, making the center of the crêpe thicker.)

Immediately place the pan on the burner and cook until the bottom side of the crêpe just begins to get brown spots. With a rubber spatula, carefully turn the crêpe over and continue to cook for about 2 minutes, until it is browned in a few places but not crisp. (If the crêpe is too crisp, it will not roll or fold easily when filled.)

Transfer the crêpe to a wire rack or plate to cool. Return the pan to the burner, adjust the temperature if the first crêpe browned too slowly or quickly, stir the batter, and rebutter or spray the pan lightly before making the next crêpe.

You may choose to fill the crêpes as they are cooked or to cool and place them between layers of waxed paper on a plate. If making them ahead, wrap and refrigerate them for 1 to 2 days, or freeze for later use. Thaw frozen crêpes on paper towels, which will absorb moisture and prevent the filled crêpes from being soggy. If using the thawed crêpes in a dessert, briefly reheat individually in a crêpe pan.

VARIATIONS

SAVORY CRÊPES: Add ½ teaspoon Dijon mustard to the batter when adding the Wondra flour.

DESSERT CRÊPES: Add 1½ teaspoons sugar and ½ teaspoon vanilla extract when adding the Wondra flour. These are particularly delicious filled with eggless vanilla ice cream and topped with chocolate sauce.

COOK'S NOTES

- Gold Medal Wondra flour is essential to this recipe; self-rising flour and all-purpose flour cannot be substituted.

- If the pan is greased too much, the crêpes will be too crisp and not pliable, and the centers will be underdone.

SPINACH CRÊPES

*Filled crêpes make a delightful side dish that can be made
ahead of time. This is one of my favorite crêpe dishes, but
a variety of fillings such as ham and asparagus, sautéed
mushrooms, ratatouille, or tomato and pesto work
beautifully as well. The cheese sauce also complements
cauliflower or broccoli and is nice on poached white fish.*

Makes 6 spinach crêpes

6 Crêpes (page 82)

CHEESE SAUCE

3 tablespoons butter
3 tablespoons flour
½ teaspoon salt
¼ teaspoon freshly ground pepper
1¾ cups milk
½ cup grated Jarlsberg or Swiss cheese

SPINACH FILLING

2 (10-ounce) packages frozen chopped spinach
2 tablespoons chopped green onions (including green portion)
2 tablespoons butter
1 teaspoon salt
¼ teaspoon grated nutmeg
Dash of Tabasco sauce
1 teaspoon Ener-G Egg Replacer, whisked with 1½ tablespoons water until foamy
Melted butter, for brushing tops of crêpes

CHEESE SAUCE: In a small saucepan over medium heat, melt the butter and stir in the
flour, salt, and pepper. Whisk in the milk and continue cooking until the sauce thickens

and comes just to a boil. Reduce the heat to medium low, then add the cheese and stir until melted. Immediately remove from the heat and set aside, or cover and chill if making ahead.

SPINACH FILLING: Defrost the spinach and squeeze it dry. Sauté the spinach and green onions in the butter until the spinach is dry and partially cooked. Add the salt, nutmeg, Tabasco, and egg replacer mixture to the spinach mixture. Blend in ½ cup of the cheese sauce; cool the filling to room temperature.

Preheat the oven to 350 degrees. Grease a 9-by-13-inch baking dish.

To assemble the crêpes, spoon ½ cup of the spinach filling in a ribbon down the center of each crêpe and roll it up. Place crêpes seam side down in a single layer in the baking dish. Brush the tops lightly with butter. (At this point you may hold the crêpes, covered, in the refrigerator for several hours.)

Bake uncovered for about 15 minutes, or until heated through, golden brown, and crisped on the edges. (If you've prepared the crêpes ahead and chilled them, cover the pan with foil and bake for 15 minutes, then remove the cover and bake for an additional 15 minutes, or until heated through and golden brown.)

While the crêpes are baking, slowly reheat the remaining cheese sauce. Place the warm crêpes on plates and top each one with 1 tablespoon of sauce. Serve any remaining sauce separately in a small bowl.

TOMATO TART

Serve this tart with grilled meat for an alfresco summer supper, when tomatoes are at their peak.

Serves 6 to 8

1 frozen pie shell, unbaked

SAUCE

½ cup eggless mayonnaise
¼ cup packed fresh basil leaves, chopped, or 1½ teaspoons dried basil
1 tablespoon drained capers, chopped
2 cloves garlic, minced
2 teaspoons fresh lemon juice
½ teaspoon salt
¼ teaspoon freshly ground pepper
1 tablespoon olive oil
8 medium ripe tomatoes, peeled, cored, and thinly sliced
⅓ cup grated Jarlsberg or Swiss cheese
¼ cup finely grated Parmesan cheese

Preheat the oven to 400 degrees.

Partially thaw the frozen pie shell for 10 minutes on the counter at room temperature. Prick the bottom and sides with a fork, one prick per about every 2 inches. Place the shell on the middle rack of the oven and bake for 12 to 14 minutes, or until just starting to brown. Remove it from the oven and cool for 10 minutes. Reduce the temperature of the oven to 350 degrees.

SAUCE: While the shell bakes, make the sauce by combining the mayonnaise, basil, capers, garlic, lemon juice, salt, and pepper in a small bowl. Stir until well blended.

Brush the bottom and sides of the cooled, baked crust with the olive oil. Arrange half the tomato slices on the crust in overlapping layers. Spread one-third of the sauce thinly over the tomatoes, being sure to reach the edge of the pie shell. Place the remaining tomatoes in overlapping layers in the pie shell. Spread the remaining two-thirds of the sauce over the tomatoes. Mix the cheeses together in a small bowl and sprinkle on the top.

Bake for 30 minutes, or until heated through. The tomatoes will be soft but should still retain their shape. Let rest at room temperature for 10 minutes before cutting.

TOMATO AND ONION SCALLOP

*This delightful vegetable side dish is so easy to prepare—
it's the perfect accompaniment to roasted meat or baked
fish, as the combination of onions and tomatoes baked
with bread cubes provides a savory yet light counterpoint
to the meat. It has been a family favorite for years.*

Serves 6 to 8

2 tablespoons butter
½ cup soft bread crumbs
2 tablespoons butter or vegetable oil
1 medium yellow onion, thinly sliced
1½ pounds tomatoes, peeled, seeded, and coarsely chopped (about 3 cups)
½ cup soft ½-inch bread cubes
1 teaspoon granulated sugar
½ teaspoon salt
¼ teaspoon freshly ground pepper
¼ teaspoon dried thyme or oregano

Preheat the oven to 350 degrees. Grease an 8-by-8-inch baking dish with butter.

Melt the 2 tablespoons of butter in a small sauté pan. Add the bread crumbs and cook over medium-low heat until dried and lightly browned, stirring frequently. Remove from the heat and set aside.

Place the other 2 tablespoons of butter or oil in a medium sauté pan and add the onions. Cook over medium heat until soft but not brown. Spread the onions evenly over the bottom of the prepared casserole dish.

Combine the tomatoes, bread cubes, sugar, salt, pepper, and thyme or oregano in a bowl and spread over the onions. Sprinkle the reserved bread crumbs over the top. Bake uncovered for 35 minutes, or until lightly browned and the tomatoes are soft.

COOK'S NOTE

- This dish may be prepared several hours ahead and placed, covered, in the refrigerator. Uncover and return it to room temperature before baking. If other items in the oven need to be at a different temperature, this dish will accommodate a temperature adjustment of about 25 degrees, and can bake for a longer or shorter time as necessary.

FRIED RICE WITH SHRIMP

Fried rice is a great side for a main course of grilled fish or meat, or can be a main course on its own. It's extremely versatile too: vary the ingredients to suit your palate or to pair with the rest of the meal. It is best made with leftover rice that has been chilled rather than freshly cooked rice, so plan ahead if you can. This dish comes together very quickly, so make sure you have all your ingredients chopped and measured before heating your pan.

Serves 4 to 6

3 cups cooked long-grain white rice (not instant rice), at room temperature or chilled
1 tablespoon vegetable oil
1 tablespoon sesame oil
1 teaspoon peeled and grated fresh ginger
1 clove garlic, minced
6 green onions, chopped (including green portion)
½ cup shredded Napa cabbage or chopped celery
½ cup sliced water chestnuts
½ cup smoked ham, cut in small slivers (optional)
3 tablespoons soy sauce
2 cups chopped cooked, shelled shrimp (or left whole if small)
Salt and freshly ground pepper

Moisten your hands with cold water and, working over a large bowl, use them to break up and separate the individual grains of rice (otherwise the rice will not separate easily when fried).

Heat the oils in a wok or heavy sauté pan over medium-high heat. Add the ginger and garlic and stir-fry for 30 seconds (do not let them brown). Add the green onions, cabbage or celery, and water chestnuts. Stir-fry for about 3 minutes. Add the rice, ham, and soy sauce and mix well. Lower the heat slightly and taste for seasoning. Add the shrimp, add salt and pepper to taste, and stir until the shrimp are heated through. Serve immediately.

CURRIED RICE PILAF

This recipe book would not be complete without my mother's rice pilaf recipe. It is wonderful with roast lamb or pork, reheats beautifully, and holds well when dinner is delayed. It also freezes nicely.

Serves 6 to 8

4 tablespoons (½ stick) butter
1½ cups uncooked long-grain white rice
1¼ teaspoons curry powder
1 teaspoon salt
¾ cup golden raisins
3 cups chicken broth

In a heavy saucepan with a lid, melt the butter over medium heat (with the lid off). Add the rice and cook until the rice is partially browned, stirring often. Add the curry powder and salt, stirring until they are well incorporated, then add the raisins and broth. Bring barely to a boil, reduce the heat to low, cover the pan, and simmer slowly for about 30 minutes, until the broth is absorbed and the rice is tender.

Remove from the heat and stir with a fork. Place a double fold of paper towels between the lid and the pan (to absorb extra moisture). Let the rice rest for 10 minutes before serving.

BAKED ITALIAN POLENTA

*This savory side dish is a cinch to prepare and goes well with
grilled meats. The mix of savory cheeses and peppery, minty basil
is a winning combination. Be sure to use fresh basil, not dried.*

Serves 5

1 (18-ounce) roll of precooked polenta
⅓ cup shredded white cheddar or Monterey Jack cheese
¼ cup grated Parmesan cheese
1 to 2 tablespoons chopped fresh basil

Preheat the oven to 375 degrees. Grease a shallow baking dish.

Cut the polenta into half-inch slices and place in the dish, overlapping the slices a little
if necessary (but do not stack them). Combine the cheeses and basil in a small bowl,
then sprinkle the mixture on top of the polenta. Proceed to the next step, or cover and
chill for up to 8 hours.

Bake uncovered for 20 to 25 minutes, or until the edges of the polenta begin to brown
slightly. Serve with a spatula while hot.

VARIATION

POLENTA MARINARA: Omit the cheddar or Jack cheese and bake as directed. Place
two slices of polenta on a plate and top with ½ cup of hot store-bought or homemade
marinara sauce. Top each serving with 1 tablespoon grated Parmesan cheese.

REUBEN SANDWICH

*Serve this ever-popular combination of corned beef, sauerkraut,
Swiss cheese, and Russian dressing with Creamy Coleslaw
(page 60), a kosher dill pickle and, of course, mustard on the side.*

Serves 4

DRESSING

⅔ cup eggless mayonnaise
3 tablespoons ketchup
1 tablespoon prepared horseradish
½ teaspoon Worcestershire sauce
¼ teaspoon salt
Dash of freshly ground pepper

SANDWICH

¾ pound prepared corned beef, thinly sliced
8 slices rye bread
8 slices Swiss cheese
½ pound sauerkraut, excess moisture squeezed out, patted with a paper towel to dry
Butter, softened
Dijon or whole-grain mustard, for serving

DRESSING: In a small bowl, combine the mayonnaise, ketchup, horseradish, Worcestershire sauce, salt, and pepper. Stir well, then cover and chill for 1 hour so flavors blend.

SANDWICH: Preheat a griddle or large skillet while assembling the sandwiches.

Place the corned beef in a shallow baking dish, separating the slices so they lie loosely on one another. Sprinkle them with a few drops of water, cover the dish lightly with plastic wrap or wax paper, and microwave for 1 minute. Remove the cover and set aside.

Lay the bread slices out on a work surface and spread the dressing on all 8 slices. Top 4 slices of the bread with a slice of cheese each. Divide the corned beef into four portions and place one on top of each cheese slice. Top the corned beef with the sauerkraut and cover with the second slice of cheese. Close the sandwiches with the remaining pieces of bread. Lightly butter the outside surfaces of the bread.

Brown the sandwiches on the griddle, placing a heatproof plate on top of the sandwiches (this weighs them down and helps them brown evenly). When the first side is golden brown, turn each sandwich carefully with a spatula and brown it on the other side. Cut in half and serve hot, with mustard on the side.

OPEN-FACED HOT CRAB SANDWICH

These terrific sandwiches have a filling of hot crab topped with slightly melted cheese. They are easy to whip up for brunch or a luncheon; serve alongside coleslaw, a green salad, or a grapefruit and avocado salad. If fresh crab is not available, chopped shrimp or poached white fish may be substituted.

Serves 4

3 cups fresh or flash-frozen cooked crabmeat
½ cup eggless mayonnaise
¼ cup low-fat sour cream
1 teaspoon Worcestershire sauce
2 teaspoons Dijon mustard
4 drops Tabasco sauce
Pinch of cayenne pepper
4 English muffins or hamburger buns, split in half
Butter or eggless mayonnaise, for spreading on muffins or buns
1 cup grated cheddar cheese

Preheat the broiler with a rack in the top broiling position and one in the center of the oven.

Place the crab in a sieve and press down on it lightly to remove any excess moisture, then wrap the crab in a paper towel to absorb the last drops of moisture.

In a medium bowl, mix the mayonnaise, sour cream, Worcestershire sauce, mustard, Tabasco, and cayenne pepper. Add the crab, shredding the larger pieces. Stir gently with a fork to mix.

Place the split muffins or buns on a baking sheet and lightly toast them on both sides under the broiler. Remove them from the oven and spread the cut sides with a little butter or mayonnaise. Adjust the oven temperature to 400 degrees. Just before baking, spoon one-eighth of the crab filling on top of each toasted half. Top each half with ¼ cup grated cheese.

Bake about 15 minutes until the cheese is melted and the crab is hot. Serve immediately.

EGG ALERT: Be sure to use real crab; artificial crab or crab-flavored seafood products most often contain egg white.

VARIATION

To make a tuna melt, use one 12-ounce can of solid tuna, drained and flaked, instead of crab, and add 2 tablespoons chopped dill pickle to the recipe.

CHICKEN NOODLE SOUP

Chicken noodle soup never goes out of style. It's a great quick-cooking meal after a busy day, and if you make it ahead and freeze it, you can get dinner on the table even faster. Serve with salad and French bread.

Serves 8

2 medium bone-in chicken breast halves
3 carrots, peeled, cut in half lengthwise, and thinly sliced
1 yellow onion, cut in half and thinly sliced
1 (8-ounce) package eggless noodles or fettuccine
7 cups chicken stock, homemade or purchased
2 tablespoons fresh lemon juice
Salt and freshly ground pepper
Chopped parsley, for garnish (optional)

Place the chicken in a microwave-safe dish. Cover it with plastic wrap, folding back one corner to vent the steam. Use medium power (50 percent) and cook for about 15 minutes, turning occasionally, until the juices run clear when cutting into the center.

Blanch the carrots and onions in boiling, salted water for 2 minutes. After blanching, remove them with a slotted spoon and quickly immerse them in cold water to stop the cooking. Drain again and set aside. Break the noodles into 2-inch pieces and drop them into the pot of boiling water. Boil until just tender, according to package directions, and drain.

Remove the cooled chicken meat from the bones and shred the meat. Pour the chicken stock into a 4-quart pot; add the chicken and blanched vegetables. Bring to a slow boil, reduce the heat, and simmer for 10 minutes. Add the cooked noodles and simmer until heated through. Add the lemon juice and correct the seasoning, adding salt and pepper to taste. Divide between 8 warmed bowls and top with a sprinkling of chopped parsley.

EGG ALERT: Though you can avoid it by making this homemade version, be aware that almost all brands of canned chicken noodle soup contain egg noodles.

ARTICHOKE AND LEMON CHEESE SPREAD

This delicious, creamy spread has a hint of lemon and gets a boost from the unique flavor of marinated artichokes. The recipe is reprinted with permission from Cooking Class by Carol Dearth, CCP, Fork in the Road Publishers. Serve with crackers or mini toasts.

Serves 8 as an appetizer

1 clove garlic
1 (6.5-ounce) jar marinated artichoke hearts, drained
Grated zest from ½ lemon
1 teaspoon fresh lemon juice
½ teaspoon dried thyme
1 (8-ounce) package cream cheese, softened

Salt and freshly ground pepper

Food processor method: Drop the garlic through the processor's feed tube with the machine running until garlic is minced. Add the artichoke hearts; pulse until they are chopped. Add the lemon zest and juice, thyme, and cream cheese. Process to blend. Season to taste with salt and pepper.

By hand method: Mince the garlic. Chop the artichoke hearts finely. Combine the garlic, artichoke hearts, lemon zest and juice, thyme, and cream cheese in a mixing bowl. Blend well. Add salt and pepper to taste.

Spoon the cheese mixture into two 6-ounce crocks or ramekins, smoothing the tops. Cover tightly and chill. Refrigerate for up to 1 week, or freeze, tightly wrapped, for 2 months. Before serving, let the chilled spread stand at room temperature for 10 to 15 minutes to soften, then serve on a tray with crackers or mini toasts.

HOLLANDAISE SAUCE

This classic, lush, and lemony sauce is wonderful served over freshly steamed vegetables or as a topper for the Ham Benedict (page 39). This hollandaise may be stored in the refrigerator for 1 day and reheated in the microwave on one-third power or on the stovetop over very low heat.

Makes 1¼ cups

1 cup milk
¼ teaspoon dry mustard
1 (0.9-ounce) package Knorr Hollandaise Sauce Mix
4 tablespoons (½ stick) butter or margarine
1 tablespoon fresh lemon juice
Dash of cayenne pepper

In a small saucepan, combine the milk, mustard, and hollandaise sauce mix. Stir together and add the butter or margarine. Place the pan over medium-high heat and bring to a slow boil, stirring frequently. Lower the heat and simmer for 2 to 3 minutes, continuing to stir until the sauce is thickened and smooth. Remove from the heat and stir in the lemon juice and cayenne pepper. Serve immediately.

To hold the sauce before serving, place the covered saucepan in a larger pan of hot water and keep both warm over low heat. Stir occasionally. The sauce may be chilled overnight and reheated using the same method, or reheated in the microwave on low power.

BÉARNAISE SAUCE

This classic French sauce, here made eggless, is similar to hollandaise, but is flavored with shallot and tarragon instead of lemon juice. It's traditionally served with steak, but is also good with broiled fish.

Makes 1¼ cups

4 tablespoons (½ stick) butter or margarine
2 tablespoons dry white wine
¼ cup finely minced shallot or onion
2 teaspoons chopped fresh tarragon, or 1 teaspoon dried tarragon
1 cup milk
1 (0.9-ounce) package Knorr Béarnaise Sauce Mix
2 tablespoons fresh lemon juice
Dash of cayenne pepper

In a small saucepan, combine the butter or margarine, white wine, shallot or onion, and tarragon. Cook and stir over medium heat until the shallot is very soft but not browned. Strain the solids from the mixture, reserving the liquid in a small bowl and discarding the solids.

Add the milk and the béarnaise sauce mix to the same saucepan. Stir together and add the reserved liquid. Place the pan over medium-high heat and bring to a slow boil, stirring frequently. Lower the heat and simmer for 2 to 3 minutes, continuing to stir, until the sauce is thickened and smooth. Remove from the heat and stir in the lemon juice and cayenne, and serve.

To hold the sauce before serving, place the covered saucepan in a larger pan of hot water and keep both warm over low heat. Stir occasionally. The sauce may be chilled overnight and reheated using the same method, or reheated in the microwave on low power.

TARTAR SAUCE

A favorite topper for crab cakes or other seafood, this sauce hits all the flavor notes: lemon juice gives it a tartness, pickles and capers a tang, the Worcestershire a savory note, and the horseradish a little kick of heat. It's best to make this sauce by hand; using a food processor or hand mixer will make it too thin.

Makes 1½ cups

1 cup eggless mayonnaise
3 tablespoons finely chopped dill pickle
1 tablespoon fresh lemon juice
1 tablespoon Dijon mustard
2 tablespoons minced fresh parsley
1 tablespoon drained capers or green olives, chopped
2 teaspoons minced yellow onion
1 teaspoon Worcestershire sauce
½ teaspoon prepared horseradish
¼ teaspoon Tabasco sauce
Salt and freshly ground pepper

In a medium bowl, combine all the ingredients and stir to mix well. Cover and chill for several hours before serving to blend flavors.

VARIATION

For a more basic tartar sauce, combine the 1 cup eggless mayonnaise with 2 tablespoons dill pickle, the mustard, 2 tablespoons minced onion, 2 teaspoons white wine vinegar, ¼ teaspoon seasoning salt, and a dash of black pepper. Chill before serving.

AIOLI

*Aioli is basically a garlic mayonnaise, often with fresh lemon
juice added. However, the modern-day chef can add a variety
of ingredients to take it to a new level. Use the variations
below, or be as creative as you wish. It's best made a few
hours ahead of time so the flavors have a chance to blend.*

Makes ¾ cup

¾ cup eggless mayonnaise
4 cloves garlic, squeezed through a garlic press
1 tablespoon fresh lemon juice
2 teaspoons olive oil

Whisk all the ingredients in a small bowl. Cover and refrigerate for several hours before
using.

VARIATIONS

RÉMOULADE AIOLI: To the basic aioli recipe, add 2 teaspoons Dijon mustard, 1
teaspoon prepared horseradish, 1 tablespoon ketchup, and 2 tablespoons minced fresh
parsley. Stir together in a small bowl, cover, and chill. Serve with shellfish.

PESTO AIOLI: Combine 1 cup eggless mayonnaise, 3 tablespoons basil pesto sauce,
and 2 teaspoons finely shredded fresh basil. Cover and chill for at least 1 hour. Serve
with crudités.

LEMON AIOLI: Combine 1 cup eggless mayonnaise, 1 teaspoon Dijon mustard, 4
cloves pressed garlic, and 2 teaspoons fresh lemon juice. Cover and chill for at least 1
hour. Serve with a white fish.

CUCUMBER SAUCE

This sauce is divine on barbecued salmon or as a topping for a plate of sliced tomatoes. Thinned with a little extra cucumber juice, it's also a great dressing for cold poached vegetables.

Makes 1¼ cups

½ medium English cucumber, peeled, cut in half lengthwise, and seeded
¾ teaspoon salt
½ cup low-fat sour cream
½ cup eggless mayonnaise
1 tablespoon minced parsley
2 teaspoons minced yellow onion
1½ teaspoons prepared horseradish
1 teaspoon white wine vinegar
¼ teaspoon cumin (optional)
Pinch of freshly ground pepper

Coarsely grate the cucumber using a box grater and place the grated cucumbers into a sieve over a bowl. Stir in the salt. Let the cucumbers drain for 30 minutes, stirring once or twice and pressing the cucumbers with the back of a large spoon to release all the juice (make sure the bowl is catching the juice, as you'll be using some). Turn the cucumbers onto a double fold of paper towels and pat dry.

Put the cucumbers into a separate bowl, reserving several tablespoons of cucumber juice for thinning if necessary and discarding the remaining juice. Add the sour cream, mayonnaise, parsley, onion, horseradish, vinegar, cumin, and pepper to the cucumbers. Stir until combined; cover and refrigerate for 1 hour.

COOK'S NOTE

• If you don't have sour cream, you can substitute plain Greek yogurt, adding ½ teaspoon honey to the recipe.

WATERCRESS SAUCE

Watercress has an unforgettable peppery bite that pairs well with the creaminess of mayonnaise. I like to put this sauce on grilled scallops or shrimp, and sometimes I thin it with white balsamic vinegar and use it as a dressing for sliced fresh tomatoes.

Makes 1¾ cups

1 cup eggless mayonnaise
½ cup chopped watercress, firmly packed
⅓ cup chopped parsley
¼ cup chopped green onions (including green portion)
¾ teaspoon Dijon mustard
½ teaspoon dried dill
2 teaspoons fresh lime juice

Combine all the ingredients in a small food processor and pulse until just blended (flecks of herbs should remain). Chill for 1 hour to blend the flavors before serving. Use within 1 day.

COOK'S NOTE

- To mix the sauce by hand, finely mince the watercress, parsley, and green onions. Place them into a small bowl with all the remaining ingredients and blend with a whisk. Cover and chill for 1 hour before serving.

BURGER SAUCE

A tablespoon or two of this sweet and savory sauce adds real zest to a hamburger.

Makes ¾ cup

½ cup eggless mayonnaise
2 tablespoons ketchup
1 tablespoon whole-grain mustard or Dijon mustard
1 tablespoon chopped dill pickle or sweet pickle relish
1 tablespoon cider vinegar
1 tablespoon minced yellow onion
½ teaspoon granulated sugar
Dash of Tabasco sauce
Salt and freshly ground pepper

Put all the ingredients in a small bowl and stir to mix well. Cover and refrigerate for 1 hour to blend the flavors. The sauce will keep for 3 days in a tightly covered container in the refrigerator.

HONEY-MUSTARD SAUCE

Serve this sauce with chicken fingers or barbecued pork. It also makes a tasty sandwich spread. Colman's mustard is a hot mustard powder that is finely ground from mustard seeds and gives foods a nice amount of bite. If you like a spicier end product, you may add more Colman's, but be cautious: the heat of the mustard intensifies when dissolved in liquid and the sauce stands for a while. And if you can't find Colman's, a few drops of Tabasco sauce are a good substitute.

Makes ¾ cup

½ cup eggless mayonnaise
2 tablespoons Dijon mustard
1 teaspoon Colman's mustard powder
2 tablespoons honey
2 dashes Tabasco sauce
Pinch of salt
¼ teaspoon turmeric (optional)

Combine all the ingredients in a small bowl and blend thoroughly. The sauce will keep for 1 week in a tightly covered container in the refrigerator.

EGG ALERT: Although not used in this recipe, many sweet mustards and Chinese mustards contain egg yolk. Read all labels carefully.

THE MAIN COURSE

TIPS AND HINTS

- **Eggless Stuffing**: Stuffing for turkey, chicken, or pork chops usually contains egg as a binder. An easy substitute is to add 1 tablespoon of liquid and ½ tablespoon of melted butter in place of each egg in the recipe. This swap works for up to 3 eggs (usually the amount called for in the stuffing for a medium turkey). You may need to add extra seasoning to compensate for the lack of egg.

- **Crispy Stir-Fried Meat**: Stir-fried meat and poultry are often dipped in an egg-white wash and then floured for a crispy finish. An egg-free workaround is to dry the pieces of meat well with a paper towel and then coat them very lightly in cornstarch. Make sure the cooking oil is hot when you add the meat. Do not overcrowd the pan, and turn the pieces to brown them on all sides as they cook. When they are done, remove them from the pan with a slotted spoon and place briefly on a paper towel to absorb any excess oil.

- **Extra-Moist Chicken**: To add extra juiciness, marinate the chicken pieces in buttermilk for at least 1 hour (or up to 8 hours) in the refrigerator before baking or frying. Remove from the buttermilk, pat dry, and prepare according to your recipe of choice.

- **Pasta: Eggless or Not?** Fresh pasta (sold in the refrigerated section at markets) almost always contains egg. Dried pastas are most often eggless, with a few exceptions: fettuccine, pappardelle, ravioli, cannelloni, and tortellini are usually made with eggs. Read every label and substitute where necessary—for example, manicotti shells for cannelloni. Be careful of finished dishes too: even if the pasta is egg-free, the creamy layer of lasagna often contains egg, and carbonara sauce is thickened with whole egg.

- **No-Boil Pasta**: No-boil noodles are often egg-free, but as always, read the labels carefully before buying. No-boil lasagna and manicotti shells are more tender if they are treated in a hot-water bath before added to a recipe. Fill a 9-by-13-inch baking pan half full of very hot water. Separate the pasta sheets or pieces and place them in the water in a single layer or overlapping crisscross style (not stacked) for 10 to 15 minutes. Remove each piece carefully and drain on a paper towel before using.

- **Freezing Leftovers**: Small portions of leftovers are great to take to someone's home when their main course will contain egg or other allergens. Freeze individual portions of casseroles or main dishes in extra-large muffin tins or small casserole dishes so they will be handy to defrost. Once the food is frozen solid, unmold it from the container, wrap it in plastic, and label each bundle with a name and date.

GLAZED MEATLOAF

*After the meat grinder was invented in Germany in the
nineteenth century, ground meats became widely available,
making meatloaf an easy dish to put on the dinner table.
It became increasingly popular in America during the
Depression and World War II as a way for thrifty housewives
to stretch ingredients. This eggless version is great served
warm at dinner, or chilled and sliced for sandwiches.*

Serves 6 to 8

2 tablespoons vegetable oil
1¼ cups minced yellow onion
3 cloves garlic, minced
1 cup soft bread crumbs
¾ cup milk
⅓ cup minced fresh parsley
⅓ cup ketchup
1 tablespoon Dijon mustard
1 tablespoon prepared horseradish
2 teaspoons Worcestershire sauce
1 teaspoon dried oregano
1 teaspoon salt
¼ teaspoon Tabasco
Egg replacer powder of choice plus liquid to equal 2 eggs, whisked together (check
    package directions)
2 pounds lean ground beef
½ pound bulk sausage meat
⅓ cup Heinz chili sauce or ketchup
1 tablespoon firmly packed brown sugar
1 tablespoon cider vinegar

Preheat the oven to 350 degrees. Grease a flat, ovenproof baking sheet or four 3-by-6-inch loaf pans.

Heat the oil in a medium skillet. Add the onion and garlic and cook, stirring, over medium heat until soft but not browned. Set aside to cool. Mix the bread crumbs, milk, parsley, ketchup, mustard, horseradish, Worcestershire, oregano, salt, Tabasco, and egg replacer mixture in a large bowl. Stir to mix well, then add the sautéed onions to the bowl. Next, add the beef and sausage. Thoroughly mix the ingredients together using your hands or an electric mixer.

Shape the mixture into a thick loaf or into four small loaves. Place in the prepared baking pan or pans. Bake the large loaf for 1 hour; bake the small loaves for 30 minutes.

Meanwhile, mix the chili sauce or ketchup, sugar, and vinegar in a small bowl. After the 1 hour (or 30 minutes) of baking time, spread this glaze over the top of the meatloaf (dividing it between the smaller loaves if necessary), and immediately return the meatloaf to the oven for 20 to 25 minutes more (about 10 minutes for the small loaves), or until a meat thermometer inserted into the center of the loaf registers 155 degrees. Using two spatulas, immediately transfer the meatloaves to a platter and cover loosely with foil. Wait for 10 to 15 minutes before slicing, if serving hot.

MEATBALLS IN MUSHROOM GRAVY

Every country has a different version of the basic meatball.
This recipe is my family's favorite, with its combination
of well-seasoned meats and a touch of nutmeg.

Serves 6 to 8

MEATBALLS

1 cup soft bread crumbs
½ cup milk
½ teaspoon xanthan gum
3 tablespoons minced yellow onion
3 tablespoons ketchup
1 teaspoon Worcestershire sauce
2 cloves garlic, minced
½ to 1 teaspoon salt (1 teaspoon if using ground pork, ½ teaspoon if using sausage)

½ teaspoon freshly ground pepper
½ teaspoon ground nutmeg
1 pound lean ground beef
1 pound ground pork or bulk sausage
2 teaspoons vegetable oil

SAUCE

½ medium yellow onion, chopped
¼ pound cremini mushrooms, thinly sliced
1 clove garlic, finely chopped
½ teaspoon dried oregano
1 cup beef broth, plus a little extra
2 tablespoons flour
¼ teaspoon salt
A few grinds of freshly ground pepper

Preheat the oven to 375 degrees.

MEATBALLS: In a large bowl, mix the bread crumbs, milk, and xanthan gum together. Add the onion, ketchup, Worcestershire, garlic, salt, pepper, and nutmeg. Stir until well blended, then add the beef and pork. Using a handheld electric mixer, mix on low speed until blended, or combine the ingredients with two forks. (Mixing thoroughly will make for more compact meatballs, which will be helpful.) With wet hands, shape mixture into 1½-inch meatballs.

Add the oil to a medium skillet and heat it over medium-high heat. Add the meatballs and brown them on all sides, then transfer to a plate. Remove excess oil from the pan, leaving 1 tablespoon.

SAUCE: In same skillet used to brown the meatballs, add the onion, mushrooms, garlic, and oregano. Sauté over medium-high heat for 5 minutes, scraping the browned bits from the bottom of the pan. Add ¼ cup of the broth and cook until the mushrooms are softened and slightly browned. Reduce the heat to medium and remove pan from heat.

In a small bowl, stir the flour with ¼ cup more of the broth. Add this to the mushrooms and stir to combine, then add the remaining ½ cup of broth, along with the salt and pepper. Stir and simmer over low heat until slightly thickened, adding a bit more broth if necessary. Add the meatballs and simmer, partially covered, until cooked through, about 15 to 20 minutes. Serve the meatballs and gravy over steamed rice or eggless pasta noodles.

VARIATIONS

ITALIAN MEATBALLS AND SPAGHETTI: Place the browned meatballs in a greased ovenproof casserole dish. Pour 3 cups (24 ounces) prepared spaghetti sauce over the browned meatballs and stir gently to combine. Cover and place in a 350-degree oven for 30 minutes. Serve over a 1-pound box of freshly boiled eggless spaghetti. Serves 6 to 8.

MAKE-AHEAD MEATBALLS: Brown and fully cook the meatballs on the stove top. Cool and place them in a freezer container. Tightly seal and freeze. Defrost in the refrigerator and prepare with your favorite sauce. Meatballs also freeze well before browning.

COOK'S NOTE

• If you're making these meatballs without the gravy, brown them in a preheated 375-degree oven in a greased 9-by-13-inch baking pan. Roast the meatballs uncovered for 15 minutes, turn them with two forks and roast for 10 minutes longer, or until cooked through.

TURKEY MEATBALLS CATALAN STYLE

Catalonia is a region in northeast Spain on the Mediterranean Sea, and its cuisine comprises many local ingredients like olive oil, fresh vegetables, and nuts. These meatballs are covered in a flavorful tomato-and-sherry sauce and finished with toasted slivered almonds.

Serves 4

MEATBALLS

½ cup fresh bread crumbs, made from coarse country-style bread
Egg replacer powder of choice plus liquid to equal 1 egg, whisked together (check
    package directions)
3 tablespoons milk
½ cup minced yellow onion
3 cloves garlic, finely minced
¼ cup minced fresh parsley
2 teaspoons fresh minced thyme
½ teaspoon salt
Freshly ground pepper
¾ pound ground lean turkey
¼ pound ground ham or sausage meat
1 tablespoon vegetable oil

SAUCE

1 tablespoon olive oil
½ cup chopped yellow onion
2 cloves garlic, minced
¼ cup medium-sweet sherry, such as Amontillado
2 medium tomatoes, peeled, seeded, and chopped
1 cup chicken broth, divided
1½ teaspoons cornstarch
½ cup toasted slivered almonds, for garnish
¼ cup minced parsley, for garnish

MEATBALLS: Place the bread crumbs, egg replacer mixture, and milk in a medium-size bowl. Mix together with a fork. Add the onion, garlic, parsley, thyme, salt, and pepper and stir until well combined. Add the turkey and ham or sausage, then mix well. Using wet hands so the mixture won't stick, shape into small, 1-inch meatballs. Heat the vegetable oil in a large sauté pan and brown the meatballs in several batches over medium-high heat until cooked through. Leave space between the meatballs so they will brown nicely. Remove from the pan and set aside.

SAUCE: Wipe out the sauté pan used to brown the meatballs, lower the heat to medium, and add the olive oil and onion. Cook slowly until the onions are translucent. Add the garlic and cook, stirring, for 1 minute more. Add the sherry, bring to a boil briefly, and scrape up the bits in the bottom of the pan. Finally, add the tomatoes and ¾ cup of the broth. Bring to a boil and simmer for 5 minutes. Reduce the heat to medium low. In a small bowl, whisk the cornstarch with the remaining ¼ cup chicken broth and stir it into the tomato sauce. Simmer for 5 minutes, stirring occasionally, until thickened.

Add the meatballs and turn them to coat with the sauce. Cover and simmer over low heat for 10 to 15 minutes. Serve immediately, garnished with the almonds and parsley, or cool the dish before garnishing it and freeze for later use.

COOK'S NOTE

- To bake the meatballs instead of browning them in a sauté pan, place on a greased 10-by-15-inch baking sheet with low sides. Bake in a preheated 375-degree oven for 15 minutes, or until the tops are slightly brown. Using two forks, turn the meatballs and continue to cook for another 15 minutes. Add the meatballs to the sauce above and continue cooking as directed.

CHICKEN AND MUSHROOM CRÊPES

This is an elegant dish; it would be a good choice for a bridal shower or a luncheon gathering of best friends. Serve the crêpes on a bed of lightly sautéed spinach for a pop of color.

Makes 8 filled crêpes

8 finished crêpes (double the crêpe recipe on page 82 and freeze the leftovers)

FILLING

4 tablespoons (½ stick) butter
1 clove garlic, minced
2 tablespoons minced yellow onion

¾ cup thinly sliced white mushrooms
½ cup all-purpose flour
½ cup milk
½ cup whipping cream
¼ cup white wine
1 teaspoon salt
½ cup drained, coarsely chopped water chestnuts
2½ cups shredded cooked chicken

SAUCE

½ cup chicken broth
¼ cup grated Jarlsberg or Gruyère cheese
2 tablespoons minced parsley, for garnish

Preheat the oven to 350 degrees. Lightly grease an 8-by-10-inch casserole dish.

FILLING: In a sauté pan, melt the butter and sauté the garlic, onion, and mushrooms over medium heat until soft but not browned. In a small bowl, stir the flour into the milk until smooth; add the flour mixture to the mushrooms, along with the cream, wine, and salt. Stir until the mixture is smooth and begins to thicken. Continue to cook, stirring frequently, until the sauce just begins to boil. Reduce the heat to low. Pour off 1 cup of the sauce and place it in a small saucepan, then set aside. Add the water chestnuts and chicken to the mushroom sauce remaining in the sauté pan, stir to combine well, and remove from the heat.

SAUCE: Combine the chicken broth and cheese with the reserved sauce in the small saucepan and heat until the cheese is melted.

TO ASSEMBLE: Place a crêpe on a large plate and spoon ⅔ cup of chicken filling down the center. Roll up the crêpe and place it seam side down in the prepared casserole dish. Fill the remaining crêpes in the same manner. Pour the cheese sauce over the top of the crêpes. Bake uncovered for about 20 minutes, or until heated through and beginning to brown on the top and edges. Place the crêpes on warmed plates, garnish with the minced parsley, and serve.

LASAGNA

*Lasagna is said to date back to the times of the ancient Romans
and Greeks, and a take on it was published in a fourteenth century
English medieval cookbook. Whatever its origins, lasagna remains
a family favorite today. This recipe contains beef and sausage,
but there is an equally delicious vegetarian alternative below.*

Serves 4 to 6

SAUCE

½ pound ground beef
½ pound mild Italian sausage, casings removed
2 cloves garlic, minced
2 teaspoons olive oil
1½ cups prepared spaghetti sauce (from a 13-ounce jar)
½ cup canned tomato sauce
2 tablespoons chopped fresh basil
2 teaspoons chopped fresh oregano
6 eggless no-boil Ronzoni lasagna noodles
¾ cup low-fat ricotta cheese
1 teaspoon Ener-G Egg Replacer, whisked with 2 tablespoons water until foamy
2 cups shredded mozzarella cheese, divided
¼ cup grated Parmesan cheese

Preheat the oven to 350 degrees. Grease an 8-by-8-inch casserole dish.

SAUCE: In a medium sauté pan, cook the beef, sausage, and garlic in the oil until crumbly and brown. Pour off any excess fat. Add the spaghetti sauce, tomato sauce, basil, and oregano. Stir to combine. Simmer for 15 minutes, stirring occasionally. Turn off the heat and set aside.

Fill a 9-by-13-inch baking pan half full with very hot water. Separate the lasagna sheets and place them in the water. Let stand for 10 to 15 minutes to soften. Remove each piece carefully and then drain on paper towels. While the noodles are soaking, combine the ricotta, egg replacer mixture, and 1½ cups of the mozzarella in a medium bowl; set aside.

TO ASSEMBLE: Spoon ½ cup of the meat sauce over the bottom of the casserole dish, and cover with 2 sheets of pasta, side by side. (Trim the pasta sheets to fit the pan if necessary.) Cover with one-third of the remaining sauce. Drop one-third of the ricotta mixture by small spoonsful over the sauce and spread evenly.

Repeat this process twice, starting each layer with pasta. Smooth out and evenly distribute each addition of sauce and cheese. Sprinkle the remaining ½ cup of mozzarella and all the Parmesan over the top. Bake for about 30 minutes, or until heated through and just beginning to brown on top.

VARIATION

MEATLESS LASAGNA: Sauté 2 cloves of minced garlic and ⅓ cup chopped onion in 1 tablespoon olive oil until soft. Add the spaghetti sauce, tomato sauce, basil, and oregano. Stir to combine. Simmer for 15 minutes, stirring occasionally. Turn off the heat and set aside. Cook a 10-ounce package of frozen chopped spinach in the microwave according to the package directions. Drain and squeeze well to remove all liquid, then season with salt to taste and set aside. Proceed with the recipe as above, spreading the spinach over the first layer of noodles. Cover the spinach with sauce and continue with the layering.

COOK'S NOTE

- Double the recipe and freeze one portion, as frozen unbaked lasagna is a great time saver. Defrost for about 8 hours in the refrigerator and bake, loosely covered, in a 350-degree oven for 45 to 50 minutes. Alternatively, cover the frozen lasagna and place it on a cookie sheet in a 275-degree oven for 1 hour. Raise the heat to 350 degrees, uncover, and bake for about 20 minutes more.

SPINACH MANICOTTI WITH TOMATO SAUCE

Large pasta tubes are stuffed with ground beef, spinach, and cheese and baked to gooey-gooey perfection. Serve with a green salad and crusty French bread. This dish freezes well and reheats easily (see below for instructions), so it's a good contender for a make-ahead meal.

Makes 14 stuffed manicotti (Serves 7)

1 (10-ounce) package frozen chopped spinach
1 pound lean ground beef
1 teaspoon olive oil
1 clove garlic, minced
⅓ cup green onions, finely chopped (including green portion)
2 tablespoons chopped parsley
1 cup ricotta cheese
6 ounces mozzarella cheese, grated (about 1½ cups)
1 teaspoon Ener-G Egg Replacer, whisked with 1½ tablespoons water until foamy
¼ teaspoon nutmeg
½ teaspoon salt
Dash of freshly ground pepper
14 eggless manicotti shells
3 cups (one 24-ounce jar) tomato-mushroom pasta sauce or other sauce of choice
¼ cup freshly grated Parmesan cheese

Grease a 9-by-13-inch casserole dish.

In the microwave, cook the spinach until wilted. Drain well in a sieve and press out all the remaining moisture. Crumble the beef into a sauté pan over medium heat and cook until lightly browned, stirring to break up any large pieces. Remove the beef from the skillet and drain it on a paper towel. Add the oil, garlic, and onions to the sauté pan and cook until slightly soft, 2 to 3 minutes.

In a large bowl, combine the spinach, beef, garlic and onion, parsley, ricotta and mozzarella cheeses, egg replacer mixture, nutmeg, salt, and pepper. Stir to blend.

Preheat the oven to 350 degrees. Boil the manicotti as directed on the box and drain it well.

TO ASSEMBLE: Spoon a small amount of sauce into the prepared casserole dish to cover the bottom. Split one side of a cooked noodle lengthwise. Fill it with about 3 tablespoons of the spinach-meat mixture and close the shell, overlapping the edges a bit. Place seam side down in the casserole dish. Repeat until all shells have been used. Pour the remaining sauce over the manicotti.

Cover with foil and bake for 15 minutes. Remove the foil and sprinkle with the grated Parmesan cheese. Bake for 10 minutes more, or until hot in the center and bubbling around the edges.

COOK'S NOTE

- To make this dish ahead, prepare the recipe as directed, but instead of baking it, wrap the dish tightly and freeze. Before baking, thaw it in the refrigerator overnight. Cover the dish with foil and bake for 30 minutes, then remove the foil and bake for 20 minutes more, or until hot in the center and bubbling around the edges.

CRISPY FISH STRIPS WITH DIPPING SAUCE

Crushed potato chips give these "fish sticks" a satisfying crunch. And the dipping sauce combines full-flavored tomato ketchup with a little mayonnaise for smoothness, and adds soy sauce for savoriness.

Serves 4

FISH STRIPS

1 pound cod or flounder, bones and skin removed
1½ cups finely crushed potato chips

½ cup dry bread crumbs
1 tablespoon dried parsley flakes
Freshly ground pepper
1 teaspoon cornstarch
⅔ cup buttermilk
1 teaspoon Dijon mustard

DIPPING SAUCE

½ cup ketchup
1 tablespoon soy sauce
2 tablespoons eggless mayonnaise
1 teaspoon water

Preheat the oven to 400 degrees. Line a 13-by-9-inch baking pan with foil and grease generously.

FISH STRIPS: Cut the fish into strips 1 inch wide and no longer than 3 inches. Combine the potato chips, bread crumbs, parsley, and pepper in a flat-bottomed bowl. In a small bowl, dissolve the cornstarch in the buttermilk and whisk in the mustard.

Dip the fish strips into the buttermilk mixture and shake off any excess. Roll them in the potato chip mixture and place in the prepared pan, leaving space between each piece. Bake for about 12 minutes, just until golden and crisp. Remove with a spatula and serve hot, with a bowl of the dipping sauce.

DIPPING SAUCE: While the fish bakes, whisk together the ketchup, soy sauce, mayonnaise, and water until blended.

COOK'S NOTE

- You'll probably have some leftover buttermilk, but don't throw it away. To use it for other recipes (like Baked Chicken Strips, page 118, Buttermilk Pancakes with Blueberries, page 44, or Panna Cotta, page 164), you can freeze it in ½-cup or 1-cup containers. Thaw it in the refrigerator, shake well, and use as needed.

BAKED CHICKEN STRIPS

Adults and kids alike will enjoy this lighter take on chicken strips. They're baked, not fried, but you won't notice the difference. The savory chicken goes well with the sweet honey-mustard dipping sauce. (For a spicier honey-mustard sauce, use the recipe on page 101.) Double or triple this easy recipe for a crowd.

Serves 6

DIPPING SAUCE

1 cup eggless mayonnaise
⅓ cup Dijon mustard
2 tablespoons honey
½ teaspoon salt

CHICKEN STRIPS

1¼ pounds boneless, skinless chicken breast halves
1 cup buttermilk
2 teaspoons Dijon mustard
3½ cups cornflakes
3 teaspoons dried parsley
¼ cup Parmesan cheese
½ teaspoon garlic salt
¼ teaspoon dried sage
1 teaspoon paprika

DIPPING SAUCE: To make the sauce, put the mayonnaise, mustard, honey, and salt into a small bowl and stir to combine. Cover the bowl and chill for 1 hour so the flavors will blend.

CHICKEN STRIPS: Gently pound the chicken breasts between two sheets of plastic wrap until they're ½ inch thick. Cut into strips ½ inch wide. In a medium bowl, add the buttermilk and whisk in the mustard. Add the chicken strips to the buttermilk mixture.

Stir to coat, cover the bowl, and chill for 30 minutes. Put the cornflakes and parsley in a plastic zip-top bag; seal the bag and crush the cornflakes with the heel of your hand until you have crumbs. Pour them into a bowl and stir in the cheese, garlic salt, sage, and paprika. Mix well to blend the spices.

Preheat the oven to 375 degrees. Line a baking sheet (large enough to fit the strips without crowding) with foil and spray it with cooking spray. Bring the dipping sauce out of the refrigerator to warm to room temperature.

Remove each chicken finger from the buttermilk and shake off the excess. Roll each piece in the cornflake crumbs and place on the prepared baking sheet. Bake for 10 to 12 minutes, or until the coating is crisp and the chicken gives a little when pressed. Do not overbake the chicken, as it will continue to cook after being removed from the oven.

Serve hot or at room temperature, with a bowl of the dipping sauce on the side.

THE COOKIE JAR

TIPS AND HINTS

- **Measuring Precisely**: Baking cookies is not difficult, but for best results bring all ingredients to room temperature before mixing and measure ingredients precisely.

- **Creaming the Butter and Sugar**: If the butter and sugar are creamed too long, the mixture will become oily, and the cookies will spread too much when baked. A general rule of thumb is to beat the butter and sugar just until the mixture has become light colored and creamy, scraping the sides of the bowl periodically.

- **Preventing Spreading**: Eggless drop cookies have a tendency to spread because they don't have egg to bind them, but they will spread less on a parchment-lined or Teflon cookie sheet than on a shiny buttered cookie sheet. (Though if you don't have parchment or a Teflon cookie sheet, greasing the pan will do in a pinch.) Allow plenty of space between drop cookies. Chilling the dough for 1 hour before baking also helps the cookies keep their shape.

- **Portioning Drop Cookies**: A small ice cream scoop is ideal for scooping chilled cookie dough onto the baking sheet.

- **Shaping Refrigerator Cookies**: Wrap a roughly formed log of dough loosely in plastic wrap and place it on the shelf of the refrigerator. Chill the log for about 25 minutes, or until it feels slightly firm. Lay the wrapped log of dough on the counter and roll it back and forth until it is even and achieves the desired diameter. Square off the ends so you have an evenly shaped cylinder. (You can also slit a paper towel core lengthwise and use it to help roll the plastic-wrapped dough inside.) Place the wrapped cookie dough directly onto the refrigerator shelf and chill it for at least 2 hours before slicing and baking. The dough may also be wrapped tightly in another layer of plastic wrap and frozen.

- **Checking for Doneness**: Check the cookies in the oven 2 to 3 minutes before the suggested baking time ends; sometimes things go faster than planned! Remove the cookies from the oven while they are still moist and slightly soft in the middle, as they will continue to cook for 10 minutes or so while resting on the cookie sheet.

- **Freezing Unbaked Dough**: Keep well-wrapped cookie dough in the freezer for up to 2 months. Thaw the dough slightly in the refrigerator, then shape or slice and bake as directed.

- **Using Sweet Crumbs**: Place eggless sugar cookies or large cubes of left-over unfrosted cake in a flat pan in a 250-degree oven for 20 to 25 minutes, or until they are very crisp but not browned. Cool and place them in the bowl of a food processor or a blender, and pulse to make fine crumbs (or crush in a sealed plastic bag). Store the crumbs in a tight-lidded jar in the freezer, and use them to sprinkle on parfaits and puddings. For crisper crumbs, or to refresh ones that have staled a bit, place them on a baking sheet in a 350-degree oven and toast until crisp, about 5 minutes.

OLD-FASHIONED CHOCOLATE CHIP COOKIES

Do you remember grandmother's chocolate chip cookies? Well, here they are, but without eggs! You'll want to keep an extra batch in the freezer.

Makes 4 dozen cookies

1 cup (2 sticks) butter, softened
¾ cup granulated sugar
¾ cup firmly packed brown sugar
1½ teaspoons vanilla extract
1 tablespoon Ener-G Egg Replacer, whisked with 3 tablespoons water until foamy
2¼ cups all-purpose flour
1 teaspoon baking soda
1 teaspoon salt
¼ cup quick oats
2 cups semisweet chocolate chips

Preheat the oven to 375 degrees. Grease a cookie sheet or line it with parchment paper.

Combine the butter, sugars, and vanilla in a mixing bowl or the bowl of an electric stand mixer; beat until fluffy and well blended. Add the egg replacer mixture to the butter mixture and beat until just blended.

Sift the flour, baking soda, and salt together. Add these ingredients plus the oats to the butter mixture and beat until partially combined. Add the chocolate chips. Mix until just blended.

Drop the dough by tablespoons onto the prepared cookie sheet. Let the cookies rest for 5 minutes before putting in the oven. Bake for about 12 minutes, or until lightly browned but still slightly soft in the center. Cool on the cookie sheet for 10 minutes before transferring to a wire rack. When the cookies are at room temperature, store in an airtight container.

VARIATION

CHOCOLATE CHIP BARS: Add 2 tablespoons milk or water to the butter mixture when creaming, then mix as for cookies. Spread the batter evenly in a greased and floured 9-by-13-inch cake pan. Bake in a preheated 350-degree oven for about 20 minutes, or until very light brown and slightly soft in the middle. Remove from the oven and cool the pan on a wire rack for 10 minutes. Cut into bars (whatever size you wish). Cool completely in the pan before removing the bars with a spatula. The bars may be stored in an airtight container for up to 3 days, then frozen for 1 month.

COOK'S NOTE

- The cookie dough will spread less when baked if the dough is chilled for at least 30 minutes before portioning the cookies.

OATMEAL COOKIES

These all-time favorites will disappear out of the cookie jar before you know it. Luckily, the dough for these chewy cookies is quick and easy to make in a food processor (or by hand).

Makes 3 dozen cookies

1 cup all-purpose flour
1½ teaspoons baking powder
1½ teaspoons Ener-G Egg Replacer powder
½ teaspoon baking soda
½ teaspoon salt
½ cup granulated sugar
½ cup firmly packed brown sugar
2 teaspoons grated orange zest
½ cup (1 stick) cold butter, cut into 8 pieces
1 teaspoon vanilla extract
¼ cup orange juice
¼ cup milk
1¾ cups old-fashioned rolled oats

¾ cup golden raisins

Grease a cookie sheet or line it with parchment paper.

In the bowl of a food processor, combine the flour, baking powder, egg replacer powder, baking soda, salt, and sugars. Pulse 3 times to blend. Add the orange zest and butter. Pulse about 12 times, or until the mixture resembles coarse meal, scraping the sides of the bowl once or twice. Add the vanilla, orange juice, and milk, and pulse several times until barely blended, scraping the bowl as needed. Add the oats and raisins and pulse about 3 times until just blended. Remove the dough from the processor, form it into a ball, then flatten the ball into a disk. Wrap it in plastic wrap and chill it for 30 minutes.

Preheat the oven to 350 degrees.

Roll the dough into 1-inch balls and place onto the prepared cookie sheet. Flatten each ball slightly with your palm, then bake for 11 to 13 minutes. The cookies should have slightly soft centers and be very light brown. Cool on the cookie sheet for 10 minutes then transfer to a wire rack to finish cooling.

VARIATIONS

CRANBERRY-OATMEAL COOKIES: Substitute 1 cup chopped, dried cranberries and 1 teaspoon grated lemon zest for the raisins and orange zest.

DATE-OATMEAL COOKIES: Substitute 1 cup chopped dates for the raisins and omit the orange zest.

COOK'S NOTE

- To mix the dough by hand, let the butter warm to room temperature. Place the soft butter, granulated sugar, and brown sugar into a large bowl. Beat with a large spoon or use a handheld mixer and beat until fluffy. Add the flour mixture along with the remaining ingredients and stir until combined.

GLUTEN-FREE OATMEAL COOKIES

Gluten-free, dairy-free, egg-free . . . and still a delicious treat!
I like Bob's Red Mill gluten-free flour for these cookies, but
you can experiment with other gluten-free baking mixes.

Makes 3 dozen cookies

1 cup plus 1 tablespoon Bob's Red Mill Gluten Free 1-to-1 Baking Flour
2 teaspoons baking powder
½ teaspoon baking soda
½ teaspoon cornstarch
½ teaspoon salt
½ cup granulated sugar
½ cup firmly packed brown sugar
2 teaspoons grated orange zest
½ cup (1 stick) cold butter or margarine, cut into 8 pieces
1½ teaspoons vanilla extract
3 tablespoons orange juice
1¾ cups old-fashioned rolled oats
¾ cup golden raisins

Grease a cookie sheet or line it with parchment paper.

In the bowl of a food processor, combine the flour, baking powder, baking soda, corn-starch, salt, and sugars. Pulse 3 times to blend. Add the orange zest and butter or margarine. Pulse 12 times, or until the mixture resembles coarse meal, scraping the sides of the bowl a few times. Add the vanilla and orange juice and pulse several times until barely blended, scraping the bowl as needed. Add the oats and raisins and pulse 3 times until just blended. Remove the dough from the processor, form it into a ball, then flatten the ball into a disk. Wrap it in plastic wrap and chill it for 30 minutes.

Preheat the oven to 350 degrees.

Roll the dough into 1-inch balls and place them onto the prepared cookie sheet. Flatten each ball slightly with the palm of your hand, then bake for 11 to 13 minutes. The cookies should have slightly soft centers and be very light brown. Leave on the cookie sheet for 10 minutes before transferring them to a wire rack to finish cooling. The cookies will get crisper as they cool.

COOK'S NOTES

- To mix this dough by hand, let the butter or margarine warm to room temperature. Place the soft butter or margarine, granulated sugar, and brown sugar into a large bowl. Beat with a large spoon or use a handheld mixer and beat until fluffy. Add the flour mixture along with the remaining ingredients and continue stirring until well mixed.

- To make other recipes in this book gluten-free, try substituting gluten-free flour mixes using the equivalent proportions suggested on the package. Depending on the grain and grind, you may need to increase or decrease the amount of liquid. There is no handy rule of thumb for these changes—you may have to try a recipe several times, adjusting its proportions, before coming up with that perfect version. Be creative.

OATMEAL MORSELS WITH RUM FROSTING

These are favorites to have on hand for a cookie tray. If you are serving children, you can substitute orange juice for the rum in the frosting.

Makes 3 dozen cookies

1 cup (2 sticks) butter, softened
½ cup sifted confectioners' sugar
½ teaspoon salt
2 teaspoons vanilla extract
2 cups all-purpose flour
1 cup quick oats
¾ cup sifted confectioners' sugar

About 2 tablespoons rum or orange juice

Preheat the oven to 325 degrees. Grease a cookie sheet or line it with parchment paper.

To make the cookies, cream the butter and the ½ cup confectioners' sugar in an electric mixer until light and fluffy. Add the salt and vanilla, then beat in the flour and oats until just mixed. Gather the dough into a large ball, ensuring that it is equally mixed and is holding together.

Roll the dough into walnut-size balls. Place the balls onto the prepared cookie sheet and bake for about 24 minutes, or until they darken very slightly. Transfer the cookies to a wire rack and cool slightly before frosting.

While the cookies are baking, make the frosting. Put the ¾ cup confectioners' sugar into a small bowl and stir in enough rum or orange juice to make a spreadable frosting. Using a pastry brush, brush the frosting onto the slightly cooled cookies. It will put a flavorful glaze on these round cookies.

VARIATION

CANDY CANE COOKIES: Roll about 2 tablespoons of the dough into a 5-inch-long stick and bend it into the shape of a candy cane. Carefully place it on a prepared cookie sheet and decorate with small slices of candied cherries. Repeat with the remaining dough to make about 24 cookies. It is best not to place cherries in the bend of the cane, as the cookies will break more easily. Bake for 18 to 20 minutes, or until they darken very slightly. Cool on the cookie sheet, then frost as detailed above. Serve the cookies right away or store them in a flat, covered container with wax paper between the layers. Handle with care!

REFRIGERATOR
SUGAR COOKIES

These crisp, easy-to-make cookies have a wonderful vanilla flavor.

Makes 2½ dozen cookies

6 tablespoons (¾ stick) butter, softened
1 (3-ounce) package cream cheese, softened
⅓ cup vegetable oil
1 cup granulated sugar
1 tablespoon water
1 tablespoon vanilla extract
2¼ cups all-purpose flour
2 teaspoons baking powder
½ teaspoon baking soda
½ teaspoon salt
Granulated sugar, for topping cookies

In the bowl of an electric mixer, beat the butter, cream cheese, oil, sugar, water, and vanilla until light and fluffy. Sift the flour, baking powder, baking soda, and salt together and add them to the butter mixture. Blend slowly until just combined.

Form the dough into two long rolls about 1½ inches in diameter on separate sheets of plastic wrap. Seal the ends of the plastic wrap and chill for 1 hour in the refrigerator. Remove the rolls from the refrigerator and, while still wrapped, roll them on a work surface to smooth out any irregularities. Return the rolls to the refrigerator for another hour until firm. At this point, the dough is ready to slice and bake, or may be frozen.

Preheat the oven to 350 degrees. Grease a cookie sheet or line it with parchment paper.

Slice the dough into scant ¼-inch slices and reshape any edges that are not perfectly round. Place each slice onto the prepared cookie sheet, leaving 1 inch between the cookies. Sprinkle each cookie with a pinch of sugar.

Bake for about 12 minutes, until the centers are a little soft and the edges are beginning to brown slightly. Cool on the cookie sheet for 10 minutes before transferring to a wire rack. Store cooled cookies in an airtight container for up to 7 days before freezing.

COOK'S NOTE

- For individually shaped cookies, you can chill the dough, then roll it out on a floured board to slightly less than ¼ inch thick. Cut out your shapes with a cookie cutter. Bake as directed above, watching toward the end of the baking time to be sure the cookies don't brown too much.

CLASSIC SHORTBREAD

Everybody likes buttery shortbread! Grandmother Mom-Mom Campbell brought this recipe with her from her home in Belfast, Northern Ireland. The grandchildren knew Mom-Mom would always have this treat for them.

Makes 10 to 16 pieces

1¼ cups all-purpose flour
3 tablespoons cornstarch
¼ cup granulated sugar, plus 2 teaspoons for topping cookies
¼ teaspoon salt
½ cup (1 stick) cold butter, cut into 6 slices

Preheat the oven to 325 degrees.

Combine the flour, cornstarch, the ¼ cup sugar, and salt in a medium bowl. Add the butter and cut it into the dough with two knives or a pastry blender until it is crumbly. (You may also use a food processor to combine the ingredients, but be careful not to overwork the dough.)

Place the dough in an ungreased 8-inch square pan or a 9-inch pie pan, patting it down firmly with a spatula until the top is smooth. Sprinkle the top of the dough with the 2 teaspoons sugar and pat it down again with the spatula. Score the dough—don't cut all the way through it—in the shape desired (10 to 12 wedges for a round pan, or 16 squares for a square pan).

Bake for 15 minutes, then reduce the oven temperature to 275 degrees and bake for about 30 minutes more. The edges of the dough should not brown. Place the pan on a wire rack to cool for 5 minutes. Cut the shortbread into squares or wedges while still hot. Let the cookies cool in the pan before removing them.

VARIATIONS

LEMON SHORTBREAD: Add 1 tablespoon grated lemon zest to the dry mixture.

GINGER SHORTBREAD: Place 2 tablespoons of the measured flour in a small food processor and add 3 tablespoons of coarsely chopped candied ginger. Pulse until minced. Add to remaining ingredients and mix as above.

MOLASSES COOKIES

Bread crumbs give these cookies a moist and light texture, and the molasses lends a distinctive sweetness. My mother acquired this recipe during World War II, when both eggs and butter were rationed, and it works perfectly today as an eggless choice.

Makes 3 dozen cookies

4 to 5 slices day-old, firm white bread (but not dried out)
3 cups all-purpose flour
1 tablespoon baking powder
2 teaspoons ground cinnamon
1 teaspoon ground nutmeg
1 teaspoon ground cloves
1 teaspoon salt
½ teaspoon baking soda
1 cup unsulfured molasses (I use Brer Rabbit brand)
½ cup granulated sugar
½ cup (1 stick) margarine or butter, melted
½ cup boiling water
½ cup rolled oats
1 cup confectioners' sugar, sifted, placed in a small paper bag

Preheat the oven to 375 degrees. Grease a cookie sheet or line it with parchment paper.

Remove the crusts from the bread slices. Make bread crumbs by using the coarse holes of a box grater to grate the bread into very coarse crumbs. You need 1 cup of crumbs.

Sift the flour, baking powder, cinnamon, nutmeg, cloves, salt, and baking soda together. Combine the molasses, granulated sugar, margarine or butter, and water in a large bowl. Add the flour mixture and beat until well mixed. Add the oats and bread crumbs, then stir to combine. Cover the dough with plastic wrap and let it rest for 30 minutes before baking so the crumbs can absorb the liquid. If a thicker cookie is desired, chill the dough for 2 hours.

Drop the dough by tablespoons onto the prepared cookie sheet. Bake for 11 to 13 minutes, or until only slightly soft in the center. Remove the cookies from the cooking sheet two at a time and immediately drop them into the sack of confectioners' sugar. Shake gently and return the cookies to a wire rack to finish cooling. Repeat with all the cookies.

PEANUT BUTTER COOKIES

Chopped salted peanuts add extra crunch to this classic sweet treat. Serve with a tall glass of cold milk.

Makes 3 dozen cookies

1½ cups all-purpose flour
½ teaspoon baking soda
½ teaspoon baking powder
¼ teaspoon salt
½ cup (1 stick) butter or shortening, softened
1 cup creamy peanut butter
1 cup firmly packed brown sugar
1 teaspoon vanilla extract
1½ teaspoons Ener-G Egg Replacer, whisked with 2 tablespoons water until foamy
½ cup chopped salted peanuts

Sift the flour, baking soda, baking powder, and salt together and set aside.

In a large bowl, using a handheld mixer, beat the butter or shortening, peanut butter, sugar, and vanilla until well blended. Add the egg replacer mixture to the butter mixture and beat for 30 seconds. Add the flour mixture and blend until combined. Add the chopped peanuts and mix until just blended. Form the dough into a large disk and wrap it in plastic wrap. Refrigerate for 1 hour.

Preheat the oven to 375 degrees. Grease a cookie sheet or line it with parchment paper.

Form the dough into balls about 1 inch in diameter and place them onto the prepared cookie sheet. Dip a fork in flour and flatten each ball twice with the fork, making a crisscross design. Bake for about 8 minutes, or until almost firm. Do not let the cookies brown, as that means they're on their way to being burned, and they will taste bitter. Cool on the cookie sheet for 5 minutes before transferring to a wire rack. Handle with care, as they crumble easily.

COOK'S NOTE

- The wrapped dough freezes well for use at a later time. Thaw it for several hours in the refrigerator, then roll into balls and prepare as directed.

CHOCOLATE HALFWAYS

Half of each of these delicious shortbread cookies is dipped in a chocolate coating—hence the name. Use a heart-shaped cookie cutter and serve these with raspberry sorbet on Valentine's Day. A low oven and long cooking time are the secrets to ensuring that the cookies bake all the way through.

Makes 4 dozen cookies

1 cup (2 sticks) butter, softened
¾ cup confectioners' sugar
1 teaspoon vanilla extract
½ teaspoon salt
2 cups all-purpose flour
1 (12-ounce) bag semisweet chocolate morsels
1 tablespoon vegetable shortening or canola oil

Using an electric mixer, cream the butter and sugar together until fluffy, then blend in the vanilla and salt. Add the flour and mix until just combined. Form the dough into a cylinder about 1½ inches in diameter on a sheet of plastic wrap. Tightly wrap the log in the plastic and chill for 30 minutes. Remove the dough from the refrigerator and roll it, wrapped, on the counter to smooth the surface of the dough. Do your best to bring the dough to a uniform diameter. Refrigerate the dough for an additional 2 hours, or until firm enough to slice.

Preheat the oven to 300 degrees. Grease a cookie sheet or line it with parchment paper.

Remove the plastic wrap and slice the dough into pieces slightly less than ½ inch thick, reshaping the edges if necessary. Place onto the prepared cookie sheet and bake for about 20 minutes, or until the cookies are slightly soft in the center and the edges are beginning to brown just a little. Cool on the cookie sheet for 10 minutes before transferring to a wire rack.

To finish, place the chocolate morsels and the shortening or oil in a microwave-safe container and microwave on low heat until the chocolate is just melted, stirring periodically until smooth. When the cookies have cooled completely, dip half of the top sides of the cookies into the chocolate and place them onto a wire rack to let the chocolate harden. Store the cookies between layers of waxed paper in a covered container for up to 7 days.

VARIATION

CHOCOLATE HEARTS: Roll out the chilled dough on a floured surface to about ¼ inch thick. Cut with a heart-shaped cookie cutter and bake as above. Dip the cooled hearts halfway into the chocolate topping and place them on a wire rack until the chocolate has hardened.

COOK'S NOTE

- For quick mixing, use a food processor to make the dough. Have the butter chilled rather than at room temperature. Place the flour, sugar, and salt in the food processor and pulse 3 times to combine. Cut the butter into tablespoon-size pieces and add to the processor. Drizzle the vanilla over the flour and pulse until just combined; stop processing as soon as the dough forms a ball. Shape as directed above and bake.

WHIPPED SHORTBREAD

*My sister, Mary Ellen, bakes delicious cookies, and she gave me
this recipe. Don't skimp on the 10 minutes of beating the dough—it
makes the cookies light and fluffy. This recipe doubles easily, and
these cookies are wonderful served with fresh fruit or sorbet.*

Makes 3 dozen small cookies

1 cup (2 sticks) butter, softened
½ cup unsifted confectioners' sugar
1 teaspoon vanilla extract or almond extract
1½ cups all-purpose flour

Preheat the oven to 350 degrees. Grease a cookie sheet or line it with parchment.

In the bowl of an electric mixer, add the butter and sugar. Beat until fluffy, then add the vanilla or almond extract and flour. Beat on medium speed for 10 minutes. Drop by small tablespoonsful onto the prepared cookie sheet.

Bake for 10 to 12 minutes, or until the bottoms are lightly browned. These cookies will flatten when baked and are crisper and less dense than typical shortbread.

CINNAMON CRISPS

*Prepared pizza dough is my secret for these sweet, cinnamony
treats. Cut into wedges, these crisps look just like pizza too!
Kids love to help make them and can't get enough of them.*

Makes 8 to 10 cookies

1 (6.5-ounce) package pizza dough mix (I use Betty Crocker brand)
1 tablespoon butter, melted
2 tablespoons granulated sugar
2 teaspoons cinnamon

Preheat the oven to 450 degrees.

Mix and roll out the pizza dough as directed on the box. Place it on a pizza pan or baking sheet and brush the top with the butter. Mix the sugar and cinnamon in a small bowl, then sprinkle the mixture over the pizza dough. Bake for 12 to 15 minutes, or until crisp but not overly browned.

Cut into wedges while hot. The cookies will crisp as they cool.

SESAME CHRISTMAS WREATHS

Shaped like a wreath, filled with bright red jelly, and studded with sesame seeds, these soft butter cookies are showstoppers on a holiday cookie tray.

Makes 3 dozen cookies

1 cup (2 sticks) butter, softened
¼ cup granulated sugar
1 teaspoon lemon extract
½ teaspoon salt
1¾ cups plus 2 tablespoons flour
⅔ cup sesame seeds
¼ cup red jelly or berry jam

Preheat the oven to 400 degrees. Grease a cookie sheet or line it with parchment paper.

In the bowl of an electric mixer, cream the butter and sugar together until well blended. Stir in the lemon extract and salt, then add the flour and mix well. Shape the dough into balls about 1 inch in diameter and place onto the prepared cookie sheet. Press your thumb into the center of each cookie to make a depression for the jelly.

Place the sesame seeds in a small bowl. Dip the top of each cookie lightly into the seeds and return it to the prepared cookie sheet. Fill the depression with a scant ¼ teaspoon of jelly or jam. It is important to not overfill with jam, as the jam will boil down the sides of the cookies when baked.

Bake for 10 to 12 minutes, or until slightly darkened.

Cool the cookies for several minutes on the pan before transferring them to a wire rack to cool completely. These cookies are best the first few days after baking; they also freeze well, so if keeping longer or making ahead, freeze them in an airtight container.

VARIATIONS

SESAME-FREE WREATHS: Use ¾ cup of crushed rice cereal or ¾ cup finely minced almonds in place of the sesame seeds.

CHOCOLATE WREATHS: Use 1 teaspoon vanilla extract in place of the lemon extract. Mix and shape the cookies as above, using the sesame seeds, but bake *without* the jelly. In a small saucepan set over simmering water (or in a microwave on low heat), carefully melt 3 ounces semisweet chocolate, 1 tablespoon butter, and 1 teaspoon corn syrup. Stir well and cool slightly. Fill each baked cookie with ¼ teaspoon of the chocolate and cool completely before serving.

COCONUT RUFFLES

Unlike other slice-and-bake cookies, these are sliced after baking. The finished cookies are crisp and have a great coconut flavor. When well wrapped, these cookies freeze well, so they are another great holiday cookie option.

Makes 9 dozen small cookies

1 cup (2 sticks) plus 2 tablespoons butter, softened
1 cup granulated sugar
1 cup finely grated unsweetened coconut
2¾ cups sifted all-purpose flour
2 tablespoons rum or fresh lemon juice
¾ cup sifted confectioners' sugar

Preheat the oven to 400 degrees. Line a cookie sheet with parchment paper.

In the bowl of an electric mixer, cream the butter and granulated sugar until light and fluffy. Blend in the coconut and then add the flour. Beat until just combined.

Divide the dough into quarters and place each piece on a floured board. Form each into a log about ¾ inch in diameter; place each dough log onto the prepared baking sheet. Press your forefinger into the dough at a slight angle to within ¼ inch of the bottom of the log. Repeat down the log of dough to form parallel ridges, like waves. Repeat with the remaining portions of dough, leaving space between the logs so they may be cut into pieces while on the baking sheet after baking. Bake the logs for 8 to 10 minutes, or until very lightly browned.

While the cookies bake, combine the rum or lemon juice with the confectioners' sugar.

Remove the logs from the oven, immediately brush with the frosting, and slice through the logs diagonally on the top of each ridge to separate each cookie into a half tunnel shape, while still hot and on the cookie sheet. Transfer the cookies to a wire rack to cool.

RASPBERRY BARS

These easy bars are great on their own as a snack, but can be made into a quick and impressive dessert by adding fresh, ripe raspberries, cutting the bars into 2-inch squares, and serving them warm with a scoop of vanilla ice cream (see Variations that follow).

Makes 18 to 24 small bars

1½ cups rolled oats
½ cup firmly packed brown sugar
¾ cup sifted all-purpose flour
½ teaspoon salt
⅔ cup soft vegetable shortening
½ cup raspberry jam

Preheat the oven to 350 degrees. Grease an 8-inch square baking pan.

In a bowl, combine the oats, sugar, flour, salt, and shortening. Beat with a handheld electric mixer or wooden spoon until thoroughly blended and crumbly. Spread two-thirds of the mixture into the prepared pan and pat down slightly. Carefully spread the jam to within ¼ inch of the edge of the pan. Crumble the reserved oat mixture over the jam and gently pat the topping with a flat metal spatula.

Bake for 35 to 40 minutes, or until the oats on top are lightly browned. Cool completely before cutting into bars.

VARIATIONS

APRICOT BARS: Substitute ½ cup apricot jam for the raspberry jam, and sprinkle ⅓ cup chopped almonds over the jam before adding the topping.

FRESH RASPBERY BARS À LA MODE: Stir 1 cup of fresh raspberries into the jam, partially crushing the berries. Spread over the oat mixture and top with the remaining mixture. Bake for 35 to 45 minutes. Cut into 9 squares and top each serving with a scoop of eggless vanilla ice cream.

BISCOTTI WITH CHOCOLATE BITS

Biscotti are wonderful with a cup of coffee or tea, and the chocolate chips make this recipe irresistible. You can also add ¼ cup of shelled pistachios or finely chopped walnuts for extra crunch. Bet you can't eat just one piece!

Makes 12 biscotti

¼ cup currants or chopped seedless raisins
2 tablespoons butter, softened
¾ cup plus 2 tablespoons granulated sugar
1 tablespoon brandy, or 2 teaspoons vanilla extract
1 teaspoon grated orange zest
1 cup all-purpose flour

¾ teaspoon baking powder
¼ teaspoon salt
1½ teaspoons Ener-G Egg Replacer, whisked with 1 tablespoon water until foamy
¼ cup mini chocolate chips

Put the currants or raisins in a small bowl. Cover with warm water and soak until softened, about 30 minutes.

Preheat the oven to 350 degrees. Grease a cookie sheet or line it with parchment paper.

In the bowl of a stand mixer, beat the butter and sugar until light and fluffy. Add the brandy or vanilla and orange zest and beat for 1 minute. Sift the flour, baking powder, and salt together. With the mixer on low speed, add the egg replacer mixture to the butter mixture, then add the dry ingredients. Mix until barely blended, scraping the sides of the bowl. Drain the currants well, discarding the liquid, and add to the dough along with the chocolate chips. Do not overmix.

Flour your hands and gather the dough together on a floured surface. Shape the dough into a 6-by-3½-inch loaf, and place onto the prepared cookie sheet. Bake the loaf until almost firm to the touch, about 30 to 35 minutes, but do not let it get too brown. After removing it from the oven, turn the oven down to 275 degrees. Let the biscotti cool for at least 30 minutes.

Move the loaves onto a cutting board and, using a serrated knife, cut the loaf into 12 (½ inch) slices. Place the slices on their sides, then return them to the cookie sheet. Bake again for about 15 minutes to dry out. Watch carefully so the slices do not get too brown and hard. They should still be a little soft in the center; they'll become crisper as they cool.

COOK'S NOTE

- If you don't have a stand mixer, use an electric handheld mixer to cream the butter and sugar, and then add the flavorings and egg replacer mixture. Stir in the dry ingredients by hand, then stir in the currants and chocolate chips.

LEMON-CRANBERRY BISCOTTI

Serve these tangy biscotti with fresh, sweetened ricotta cheese for dessert. You'll get the best results if you chill the dough overnight before baking—the flour will absorb the liquid and the dough will hold together better.

Makes 16 biscotti

2 cups all-purpose flour
1 teaspoon baking powder
½ teaspoon nutmeg
½ teaspoon salt
½ cup (1 stick) butter, softened
1 cup granulated sugar
1 tablespoon grated lemon zest
1½ teaspoons Ener-G Egg Replacer, whisked with 2 tablespoons fresh lemon juice until foamy
2 tablespoons orange juice
1 cup dried cranberries

Sift together the flour, baking powder, nutmeg, and salt.

Put the butter and sugar in the bowl of a stand mixer and beat until light and fluffy. Stir in the lemon zest. Add the egg replacer mixture and beat just enough to blend into the butter mixture. Add half of the flour mixture and mix to combine. Add the orange juice and mix briefly, then add the remainder of the flour mixture. Stir until barely blended. Mix in the cranberries.

Divide the dough and form it into two slightly rounded loaves, about 4 by 8 inches and less than 1 inch in thickness; wrap the loaves in plastic wrap. Chill for at least 3 hours or overnight.

Preheat the oven to 325 degrees. Grease a cookie sheet or line it with parchment paper.

Place the two loaves onto the prepared baking sheet. Cover with plastic wrap and bring to room temperature. Remove the plastic wrap and bake for 30 to 40 minutes, or until lightly browned and still soft in the center. Remove from the oven, then turn the oven down to 275 degrees. Let the biscotti cool for 30 minutes.

Move the loaves onto a cutting board and, using a serrated knife, cut each loaf into 8 (½ inch) slices. Place the slices on their sides, then carefully return them to the cookie sheet. Bake for about 15 minutes. The centers should still be a little soft; they will become crisp when cool.

BROWNIES WITH CHOCOLATE FROSTING

This brownie is exceptionally moist, thanks to yogurt and sour cream, and chocolate frosting gives it extra fudgy goodness. Wrap any leftovers in plastic and freeze them.

Makes about 32 brownies

BROWNIES

1¾ cups all-purpose flour
1¾ cups granulated sugar
¾ cup unsweetened cocoa powder
2 teaspoons baking powder
¼ teaspoon salt
½ cup (1 stick) butter, melted and cooled
½ cup plain low-fat yogurt
½ cup low-fat sour cream
2 teaspoons vanilla extract
⅔ cup semisweet chocolate chips
Confectioners' sugar (optional, to dust on top if not using frosting)

FROSTING

3 cups confectioners' sugar
⅔ cup unsweetened cocoa powder
½ cup (1 stick) butter, melted and slightly cooled
⅓ cup milk
1 teaspoon vanilla extract

Preheat the oven to 350 degrees. Grease a 9-by-13-inch baking pan or two 8-by-8-inch baking pans. Line them with parchment paper, grease the paper, and dust with flour.

BROWNIES: In a large bowl, sift the flour, sugar, cocoa, baking powder, and salt together. Add the butter, yogurt, sour cream, and vanilla to the flour mixture and stir by hand until well combined. The dough will be very stiff. Stir in the chocolate chips, then spread the dough into the prepared pan.

Bake for 35 to 40 minutes for the 9-by-13-inch pan; bake for 20 to 25 minutes for the 8-by-8-inch pans. A toothpick inserted in the center should come out clean. Remove from the oven and cool in the pan on a wire rack.

When completely cool, run a table knife along the edges of the pan, loosen the paper, then place a wire rack over the top of the pan and quickly flip it over. The brownies will come out onto the rack. Peel off the parchment paper, put a second wire rack onto the bottom of the brownies, and flip them over once more.

FROSTING: Sift the confectioners' sugar and cocoa together in a medium bowl. Add the butter, milk, and vanilla; beat until smooth. Add more milk if necessary. Spread the frosting evenly over the surface of the brownies. After the frosting has hardened, cut the brownies into squares. Store in an airtight container with parchment or wax paper between layers if not serving immediately. If not using frosting, dust with confectioners' sugar.

THE CAKE BOX

TIPS AND HINTS

- **Prepare the Pans**: To avoid sticking, it is best to line a greased cake pan with parchment or wax paper, then grease and lightly flour the paper. Prepare the pan before mixing the cake so the rising action will not begin in the bowl.

- **Measure Precisely**: Be exact when measuring ingredients; spoon dry ingredients into the measuring cup, rather than scooping, and level them off with a knife. To avoid inaccurate measurements, don't measure ingredients over the mixing bowl.

- **Have the Ingredients at Room Temperature**: Cakes will be lighter if all the ingredients start at room temperature; however, the butter/shortening should not be so warm that it droops or begins to break.

- **Follow Directions Exactly**: Read the recipes thoroughly before you begin. The directions must be followed very carefully; the techniques for these recipes may be different than for other cake baking you have done.

- **Don't Overbeat the Butter**: Butter will become greasy and lose air bubbles if it is over-creamed. As a result, the cake will not rise well and will be sticky. Beat the butter or shortening until just light and fluffy.

- **Do Not Overwork the Flour**: Do not overbeat the flour with the other ingredients; this develops gluten and causes the cake to be sticky and tough. Gently mix the flour and liquid into the creamed butter/shortening and sugar until just combined and any lumps are smoothed out.

- **No Peeking**: Eggless cake batter is very sensitive to drafts. Do not open the oven door to check on the cake until the last 10 to 15 minutes of the baking time. Remember to set a timer.

- **Freezing Cakes**: Unfrosted cakes freeze nicely when completely cooled and wrapped well. Eggless cakes lose their freshness quickly, so if you don't plan to serve them the same day, it's generally better to freeze them and thaw when needed. Frosted cakes can be also frozen; to do so without creating a mess, freeze the pieces unwrapped, allowing the frosting to solidify. Then wrap well for longer storage.

- **Pan Size**: If you don't have the pan size called for, you may substitute a slightly larger pan. A smaller one will not work; the cake will be too thick and won't rise evenly. If you want a thicker cake, use a ring mold or create one by placing a narrow aluminum can, such as a tomato paste can (top and bottom removed, wrapper peeled off), in the middle of the cake pan. This will allow the heat to reach the middle of the cake.

- **Cupcakes**: Paper liners work well; spray them with a little cooking oil before pouring in the batter. Most cake batters can easily be made into cupcakes; however, it is usually best to bake cupcakes at 375 degrees and reduce the baking time by about 15 minutes.

- **Easy Layer Cakes**: For a two-layer cake, double the recipe and bake in a 9-by-13-inch cake pan, then cut the cooled cake in half (horizontally) to make a 9-by-6½-inch layer. For a four-layer cake, double or triple the recipe and pour the batter into a jelly roll pan. Cut the cake into four 6-by-9-inch quarters.

- **Packaged Cake Mixes**: Packaged cake mixes may not have eggs in the mix, but typically require several eggs in the preparation. And using an egg replacer with a packaged mix often has disappointing results because the mix is not formulated for this change. Skip the mix, take an extra 10 minutes, and make a real eggless cake that everyone will truly enjoy.

- **Texture**: It takes a bit of adjusting to get the texture of eggless cakes just right when converting an egg cake recipe, but the recipes in this book will give you a base on which to adapt your old favorites to the eggless way.

- **Cake Flour**: Cake flour can be used in place of all-purpose flour—however, note that 1 cup of all-purpose flour equals 1 cup plus 2 tablespoons of cake flour. Do not substitute self-rising flour for either all-purpose or cake flour when making cakes unless the recipe specifically calls for it.

- **Fresh Fruit**: With the exception of fresh blueberries, fresh (or frozen) fruit added to cakes typically yields too much moisture and should be avoided.

- **Last-Minute Cake**: Keep cupcakes or a spare layer of cake in the freezer so your child can take a piece of their eggless cake to a birthday party. (You can also use the layer of cake to make a last-minute dessert such as tiramisu).

- **Mess-Free Frosting**: When frosting a cake on its serving plate, place four pieces of wax paper around the edges of the cake plate, and then place the unfrosted cake in the middle of the plate, on top of the inner edges of the paper. Proceed with the filling and frosting of the cake. When finished, gently pull the wax paper away from the cake; the serving plate will be free of smeary frosting marks.

- **Leftover Cake**: Put slices of leftover unfrosted cake on a rack in a 250-degree oven until they are dry, but not browned, about 30 minutes. Top with a scoop of eggless ice cream and some dessert sauce. Or make crumbs out of the dried cake and sprinkle them on the top of ice cream for a little crunch, or use as a topping for fruit crisps.

- **Cake Decorating Ideas for Kids**: Place a parade of animal crackers at the base of the cake marching around in one direction, and a second parade going in the opposite direction on the top of the cake. Adhere the crackers with a dab of frosting on the backs just before serving the cake, so the crackers will remain crisp. Place 3 gumdrops around the base of each candle to accentuate them.

ADAPTING A CAKE RECIPE WITH EGGS TO AN EGGLESS CAKE

- When substituting egg replacer for real eggs in a recipe, check the original recipe and use only those that call for 1 cup (or more) of flour per egg used. Recipes with less than 1 cup of flour per egg are not good candidates for eggless cakes.

- Pour the batter into the pan, spread it evenly, and then let it rest for 5 minutes before placing it in the preheated oven.

- For optimal results, bake eggless cakes at 350 degrees.

- Cool cakes in the pan on a wire rack for only 5 minutes. This allows the cake to firm up, but not so much that it will be difficult to remove from the pan. Run a table knife around the sides of the cake pan to loosen the edges. Cover the pan with a rack and flip it over. Peel off the paper; immediately top with a second rack and turn it over again so the cake cools right side up. Cool completely before filling, frosting, or slicing.

YELLOW CAKE WITH RASPBERRY FILLING

*My mother created this basic eggless cake recipe without
the egg replacer, and it was my birthday cake of choice
for years. Many a time as a little girl, I sat on the kitchen
stool and creamed the butter and sugar together in a bowl
with a wooden spoon. Sunbeam introduced the home-size
electric mixer in 1930 and revolutionized cake baking in
the home. Now we make cakes in a matter of minutes!*

Serves 8 to 10

CAKE

2½ cups all-purpose flour
1¼ cups granulated sugar
2½ teaspoons baking powder
½ teaspoon salt
½ teaspoon xanthan gum
½ cup (1 stick) butter or margarine, slightly softened
2 teaspoons Ener-G Egg Replacer, whisked with 3 tablespoons water until foamy
1 cup milk
1½ teaspoons vanilla extract

FILLING AND FROSTING

½ cup raspberry jam
3 cups confectioners' sugar, sifted
¼ cup cream or milk, warmed
1 teaspoon butter, melted
1 teaspoon vanilla extract

Preheat the oven to 350 degrees (375 degrees for cupcakes). Grease two 8- or 9-inch
round cake pans or a 9-by-13-inch cake pan for an unfilled cake. Line the bottoms with

parchment or wax paper, then grease the paper and lightly flour the bottom and sides. If you're making cupcakes, line a standard-size muffin tin with paper cups sprayed with cooking oil.

CAKE: Sift the flour, sugar, baking powder, salt, and xanthan gum together in the bowl of an electric mixer or large mixing bowl. Cut the butter into 8 pieces and add to flour mixture. Beat on low speed for 1 minute until the mixture resembles fine crumbs. Turn off the mixer. Add the egg replacer mixture, milk, and vanilla. Beat at low speed for only 30 seconds, stopping to scrape the sides of the bowl several times.

Spoon the batter into the prepared pans and spread evenly. Let the batter rest for 5 minutes before baking. Bake for 25 to 30 minutes (about 15 minutes for cupcakes) or until a toothpick inserted in the center comes out clean and the cake has slightly begun to come away from the sides of the pan.

Place the pans on a wire rack to cool for 5 minutes. Run a knife around the sides of the pans to loosen the edges. Top the pan with a wire rack and flip it over, peel off the paper, and immediately top with a second wire rack and turn the cake right side up. Repeat with the other layer. Cool completely before filling and frosting.

FILLING AND FROSTING: Stir the jam a little to soften it before spreading it on the cake. Place the first layer of the cake on a serving plate, spread with the jam filling, then lay the second layer on top. If making cupcakes, omit the jam.

To make the frosting, combine the confectioners' sugar, cream or milk, butter, and vanilla in a bowl. Beat until very smooth. If necessary, add a little more milk or confectioners' sugar until it is spreadable but thick enough to not run down the sides of the cake. Use the frosting immediately; frost the sides first and the top last.

CHOCOLATE-RASPBERRY LAYER CAKE WITH FUDGE FROSTING

"I'm only going to heaven if there is chocolate cake." I don't remember where I first heard this quote, but these are words to live by!

Serves 8

CAKE

2 cups all-purpose flour

1½ teaspoons baking soda

½ teaspoon salt

2 ounces unsweetened baker's chocolate

½ cup (1 stick) butter

2 cups granulated sugar

½ cup buttermilk

1 teaspoon vanilla extract

½ cup water, at room temperature

1 tablespoon Ener-G Egg Replacer, whisked with ¼ cup water until foamy

FILLING AND FROSTING

½ cup raspberry jam

2 ounces unsweetened baker's chocolate

½ cup butter

½ cup firmly packed brown sugar

3½ cups confectioners' sugar, sifted

¼ cup sour cream

1 tablespoon light corn syrup

1 teaspoon vanilla extract

¼ teaspoon salt

Preheat the oven to 350 degrees. Grease two 9-inch round cake pans, line the bottoms with parchment or wax paper and grease again, then lightly dust with flour.

CAKE: Sift the flour, baking soda, and salt together. Melt the chocolate and butter in the microwave on half power until barely melted, stirring to mix well. In a large bowl or an electric mixer bowl, combine the sugar, buttermilk, and vanilla; beat at a low speed. Add the chocolate mixture, beating until just blended. Add the water and egg replacer mixture and mix at low speed. Add the flour mixture to the bowl and beat at low speed for 1 minute. The batter will be thin.

Pour the batter into the prepared pans. Let the batter rest for 5 minutes before baking. Bake for about 30 minutes or until a toothpick inserted in the center comes out clean and the cake springs back when pressed gently in the center. Place the pans on a wire rack to cool for 10 minutes. Run a knife around the sides of the pans to loosen the edges. Top the pan with a wire rack and flip it over, peel off the paper, and immediately top with a second wire rack and turn the cake right side up. Repeat with the other layer. Cool completely before filling and frosting.

FILLING AND FROSTING: Stir the jam a little to soften it before spreading it on the cake. Place the first layer of the cake on a serving plate, spread the jam filling on it, then lay the second layer on top.

To make the frosting, melt the chocolate and butter in the top of a double boiler (or use a heatproof bowl placed in a pan of simmering water). Keep the water simmering and add both sugars, sour cream, corn syrup, vanilla, and salt. Cook until the sugars are dissolved and frosting is glossy. Do not overcook, as it will turn into candy. Immediately frost the cake before the frosting hardens.

APPLESAUCE LAYER CAKE WITH CARAMEL FROSTING

This very special dessert was created by Margaret Steen, an outstanding lady who has catered many lovely parties, including my 50th birthday party, where she served this cake as a surprise.

Serves 8 to 10

CAKE

2 cups all-purpose flour
1 teaspoon baking powder
1 teaspoon salt
1 teaspoon cinnamon
¼ teaspoon cloves
½ cup (1 stick) butter
1 cup granulated sugar
1 cup applesauce
1 teaspoon baking soda
2 tablespoons hot water
¼ cup golden raisins
¼ cup drained crushed pineapple
½ cup brandy

FROSTING

½ cup butter
1 cup firmly packed brown sugar
¼ teaspoon salt
¼ cup milk
2 cups confectioners' sugar, sifted after measuring

Preheat the oven to 350 degrees. Grease two 9-inch round cake pans and line the bottoms with parchment; grease again and dust with flour.

CAKE: In a medium bowl, sift the flour, baking powder, salt, cinnamon, and cloves together. Using an electric mixer, cream the butter and sugar, beating well until fluffy. Add the flour mixture to the butter mixture in 3 additions, alternating with the applesauce, ending with flour. Stir the baking soda and hot water together in a small bowl and add to the batter. Stir in the raisins and pineapple. Beat slowly—no more than necessary—to just blend.

Spread the batter evenly in the prepared pans. To allow the leavening to work, let the pans stand for 5 minutes before placing them in the oven.

Bake for about 30 minutes, or until a toothpick inserted in the center comes out clean. Remove the cakes from the oven and prick them about every 2 inches with a fork. Use a pastry brush to distribute ¼ cup of the brandy over each layer and immediately turn the cakes out onto a wire rack to cool. Cool to room temperature before frosting.

FROSTING: In a small saucepan, melt the butter over low heat; stir in the brown sugar and salt. Bring to a boil and boil hard over medium heat for 2 minutes, stirring constantly. Remove from the heat and stir in the milk. Return to the heat and bring back to a full boil for just a few seconds. Cool to lukewarm.

Transfer the mixture to a medium bowl and add the confectioners' sugar, beating until smooth. If the frosting is too thick, add 1 to 2 teaspoons of milk. Immediately spread some frosting on the first layer and place the second layer on top of it. Frost the sides and then the top of the cake.

COOK'S NOTE

- One-and-one-half times the recipe will fill a 9- to 10-inch Bundt pan and will need only one recipe of frosting. For a three-layer cake, use 9-inch round pans and double the recipe for both batter and frosting.

CARROT BUNDT CAKE

This favorite fall cake holds nicely, so it is just as delicious the second day. Try it for breakfast!

Serves 6

CAKE

1½ cups all-purpose flour
1 tablespoon baking powder
1 teaspoon ground cinnamon
½ teaspoon ground nutmeg
½ teaspoon salt
1¼ cups finely shredded carrots (about 3 medium)
¾ cup firmly packed brown sugar

¼ cup granulated sugar

2 teaspoons grated orange zest

2½ teaspoons fresh lemon juice

1 teaspoon Ener-G Egg Replacer, whisked with 2 tablespoons water until foamy

1 teaspoon vanilla extract

½ cup (1 stick) butter, melted and cooled

¼ cup vegetable oil

½ cup golden raisins

ICING

1 tablespoon butter, softened

1 (3-ounce) package cream cheese, softened

2 teaspoons grated lemon or orange zest

1 teaspoon vanilla extract

⅛ teaspoon salt

2 to 2¼ cups sifted confectioners' sugar

Preheat the oven to 350 degrees. Grease and very lightly flour a 9-inch Bundt pan.

CAKE: Sift the flour, baking powder, cinnamon, nutmeg, and salt together in a large bowl. In a medium bowl, combine the carrots, sugars, orange zest, lemon juice, egg replacer mixture, and vanilla. Stir with a fork to thoroughly mix. Stir in the butter, oil, and raisins. Fold into the flour mixture until just combined. Pour the batter into the Bundt pan. Let it rest for 5 minutes before placing it into the oven.

Bake for 40 to 50 minutes, or until a toothpick inserted in the center comes out clean. Let the cake rest for 5 minutes before turning out onto a wire rack to cool. Cool completely before frosting or slicing.

ICING: Using an electric mixer, beat the butter, cream cheese, zest, vanilla, and salt in a medium bowl until well blended. Add 2 cups of the sugar and blend well. Add a little more sugar until the icing is the right consistency for spreading on the cake. If you'd rather drizzle the icing onto the cake, thin it slightly with milk.

COOK'S NOTES:

- Be sure to use a fine grater for the carrots; otherwise, the pieces of carrot will be too heavy for the batter.

- This recipe calls for a fairly small Bundt pan. Check yours—it should be about 9 inches across the top. This size pan may also be referred to as a 6-cup Bundt pan.

SPICE CAKE

*This cake, rich with cinnamon, nutmeg, cloves, and allspice,
smells and tastes like fall. I love a slice of it with a cup of coffee as
a late-afternoon treat. It stands on its own without frosting, but
if you want a little extra sweetness, sift some confectioners' sugar
over the top or serve it with a scoop of eggless maple ice cream.*

Serves 8 to 10

½ cup (1 stick) butter, at room temperature
1 cup granulated sugar
2 teaspoons Ener-G Egg Replacer, whisked with 3 tablespoons water until foamy
1 teaspoon vanilla extract
2 cups all-purpose flour
2 teaspoons baking powder
½ teaspoon baking soda
1 teaspoon ground cinnamon
1 teaspoon ground nutmeg
½ teaspoon ground cloves
½ teaspoon ground allspice
½ teaspoon salt
1 cup buttermilk

Preheat the oven to 350 degrees. Grease and lightly flour a 9-inch tube or Bundt pan.

Place the butter and sugar into the bowl of a stand mixer. Beat until lightly creamed and fluffy. Add the egg replacer mixture and vanilla; beat until just blended.

Sift the flour, baking powder, baking soda, cinnamon, nutmeg, cloves, allspice, and salt together. Add the flour mixture and the buttermilk to the butter mixture alternately in three additions. Mix at a slow speed and do not overbeat. Spoon the batter into the prepared pan and let it rest for 5 minutes before placing into the oven.

Bake for about 45 minutes, or until a toothpick inserted in the middle comes out clean. Let the cake rest for 5 minutes before turning out onto a wire rack to cool.

BANANA CAKE WITH LEMON ICING

This small cake has a unique flavor combination, and best of all, it takes under an hour to make and serve!

Serves 6

CAKE

1 cup all-purpose flour
1½ teaspoons baking powder
½ teaspoon salt
1 large banana, very ripe
½ cup granulated sugar
4 tablespoons (½ stick) butter, softened
1 teaspoon vanilla extract
2 tablespoons milk
1 tablespoon fresh lemon juice
1½ teaspoons Ener-G Egg Replacer, whisked with 2 tablespoons water until foamy
½ cup chopped toasted walnuts (optional)

ICING

1½ cups confectioners' sugar, sifted
2 tablespoons plus 1 teaspoon fresh lemon juice

Preheat the oven to 350 degrees. Grease an 8-inch square baking pan and line it with parchment. Grease the paper and dust the pan lightly with flour.

CAKE: In a small bowl, sift the flour, baking powder, and salt together. Mash the banana in a large mixing bowl and add the sugar. Mix well, using an electric hand mixer. Add the butter, vanilla, milk, and lemon juice. Mix until well combined. Add the egg replacer mixture and blend. Stir in the flour mixture; do not overmix. Fold in the walnuts by hand.

Pour the batter into the prepared pan and let it rest for 5 minutes before placing it in the oven. Bake for about 25 minutes, or until a toothpick inserted in the center comes out clean.

Let the cake cool in the pan for 10 minutes. Run a small knife around the edges of the pan, then turn the cake out onto a wire rack and invert it back (so it is right side up) onto a second rack. Cool to room temperature.

ICING: Mix the confectioners' sugar and lemon juice together until smooth. If too thin, add a little more sifted confectioners' sugar. Frost the sides first, then the top of the cake with the lemon icing.

PINEAPPLE UPSIDE-DOWN CAKE

Pineapple and upside-down cake have gone together for years.
Serve this one plain or with a spoonful of whipped cream.

Serves 6 to 8

1 (8.5-ounce) can pineapple slices
3 tablespoons butter
½ cup brown sugar
1⅓ cups all-purpose flour
⅔ cup granulated sugar
2 teaspoons baking powder
½ teaspoon salt

⅓ cup (5⅓ tablespoons) butter, softened
1½ teaspoons Ener-G Egg Replacer, whisked with 2 tablespoons water until foamy
½ teaspoon vanilla extract
⅔ cup milk
Whipped cream, for topping

Preheat the oven to 350 degrees. Grease an 8- or 9-inch square pan or a 9-inch tube pan very well. Do not line with parchment or flour the pan.

Drain the pineapple slices on paper towels, saving the juice for another purpose. Place the 3 tablespoons butter in the baking pan and place it in the oven until just melted. Remove the pan from the oven and add the brown sugar, blending it into the butter with the back of a spoon. Spread the mixture evenly around the pan bottom. Place 4 pineapple slices in the pan. (If using a tube pan, cut the slices in half and place them in a scalloped fashion in the bottom of the mold.)

Sift the flour, granulated sugar, baking powder, and salt into a mixer bowl. Add the ⅓ cup butter and beat on low speed until the flour mixture looks like coarse meal. Combine the egg replacer mixture and vanilla with the milk in a medium bowl, then pour the liquids into the mixer bowl. Beat on low speed until just blended, scraping the sides of the bowl to combine. Spoon the batter over the pineapple and spread evenly to smooth the top, working carefully so as not to dislodge the fruit slices. Let it rest at room temperature for 5 minutes before placing it in the oven.

Bake for 45 to 50 minutes, or until a toothpick inserted in the center comes out clean. Run a spatula around the edges to loosen. Immediately invert the cake onto a serving plate. *Do not lift the pan from the cake for 1 minute*; this will allow the sauce to drip into the cake. Carefully remove the pan and let the cake cool briefly before cutting into serving pieces and topping with whipped cream.

WHIPPED FROSTING

This frosting comes as close to any using whipped egg whites as you will find. Its fluffy texture is like whipped marshmallows, and it is wonderful to use on rich yellow and coconut cakes. Use it to frost cupcakes, topping each with a birthday candle.

Makes 2½ cups

¼ cup cold water
1 teaspoon unflavored gelatin powder
2 cups cold whipping cream, divided
¼ cup confectioners' sugar
½ teaspoon vanilla or lemon extract

Put the water in a small bowl and sprinkle the gelatin over it. Slightly heat ¼ cup of the cream on a low setting in the microwave. Pour the warmed cream over the gelatin and stir until it is dissolved. Refrigerate for a few minutes until it is the consistency of pancake syrup, but not completely jelled (watch it carefully).

Use an electric mixer (or a large chilled bowl and a whisk) to whip the remaining 1¾ cup cream until soft peaks form. By hand, using a wire whisk, gently fold the gelatin mixture, sugar, and vanilla or lemon extract into the whipped cream. Immediately use to frost a cake.

SIMPLE ICING

This light icing is ideal for a simple cake and must be made just before using as it sets up very quickly. For an instant treat, use it as a layer of filling between graham crackers.

Makes 1 cup

1 cup sifted confectioners' sugar
2 tablespoons milk, warmed slightly
½ teaspoon vanilla or lemon extract

Combine the sugar, milk, and vanilla or lemon extract in a small bowl and stir until smooth. Add additional sifted confectioners' sugar if the icing is too thin.

LEMON FILLING

*I've relied on this tart, tasty lemon cake filling for years.
It looks and tastes a bit like lemon curd and may be used
in similar ways. For a speedy dessert, it's also wonderful
in mini tart shells topped with a fresh raspberry.*

Makes 1½ cups

½ cup granulated sugar
2 tablespoons cornstarch
⅛ teaspoon salt
⅓ cup boiling water
2 tablespoons butter
1½ tablespoons grated lemon zest
3 tablespoons fresh lemon juice, divided
Yellow food coloring

Mix the sugar, cornstarch, and salt in a small saucepan. Place over medium heat and slowly add the water, stirring until the filling begins to thicken. Add the butter and continue stirring until the filling is clear and slightly thicker. Remove from the heat and stir in the lemon zest and juice, and 1 very small drop of food coloring. Cool to room temperature before using.

DESSERTS

TIPS AND HINTS

- **No Soggy Piecrusts**: Partially baking a pie shell and then brushing it with butter before filling with fruit will prevent the crust from becoming soggy.

- **Steamed Puddings**: Because steamed puddings are prepared a few hours before serving, they do not require last-minute attention and are perfect for winter dinners. (They may be steamed earlier in the day, unmolded and cooled, wrapped and refrigerated, then reheated, loosely wrapped, in the microwave before serving.) A designated steamed pudding mold has two important features: a tube coming up from the middle, which helps cook the pudding evenly and makes the end product lighter, and a fitted lid that fastens down tightly.

- **Equipment Options for Steamed Puddings**: If you don't have the special mold mentioned above, you can still make steamed puddings very successfully with an improvised mold in an improvised steamer—see the Steamed Cranberry Pudding with Vanilla Sauce (page 172), under Cook's Notes for tips.

PUMPKIN PIE

The early American settlers did not have ovens, so pumpkin pie did not become a holiday tradition until the late 1600s. As the story goes, Native Americans gave the Pilgrims pumpkins to roast with honey and spices for their first Thanksgiving dinner in 1621. Plan ahead when making this pie, as the filling needs to chill for at least 2 hours before continuing with the recipe.

Makes 8 servings

1½ cups (from one 15-ounce can) canned pumpkin
¾ cup firmly packed brown sugar
1 teaspoon ground cinnamon
1 teaspoon ground ginger
½ teaspoon ground nutmeg
¼ teaspoon ground cloves
¼ teaspoon ground allspice
½ teaspoon salt
1 tablespoon Wondra flour, or 1½ teaspoons cornstarch
1 unbaked 9-inch piecrust (homemade or purchased)
1½ tablespoons butter, melted
1¼ cups canned evaporated milk
1 tablespoon Ener-G Egg Replacer, whisked with 3 tablespoons water until foamy
2 tablespoons honey

Place the pumpkin in a bowl and stir in the sugar, cinnamon, ginger, nutmeg, cloves, allspice, salt, and Wondra or cornstarch until well mixed. Cover and refrigerate for 2 hours or overnight to allow the flavors to blend.

Preheat the oven to 350 degrees. Bring the pumpkin mixture to room temperature.

Prick the pie shell all over with a fork and bake it for 10 minutes, or until it just begins to change color. Check the crust after it has baked for a few minutes and, if bubbles are developing, gently prick it again with a fork. After removing the crust from the oven, brush the partially baked pie shell with the butter.

Add the evaporated milk, egg replacer mixture, and honey to the pumpkin mixture. Combine well. Pour the pumpkin mixture into the pie shell, being careful to not overfill the pie. (Leave a ½-inch space between the filling and the top of the piecrust to allow for the filling to expand as it bakes.) Bake for 30 to 40 minutes, or until the filling is set and a toothpick inserted in the center comes out clean. Serve at room temperature.

COOK'S NOTES

- If any pumpkin filling is left over, pour the remaining filling into small, greased ovenproof casserole dishes. Bake at 350 for about 20 minutes, or until a toothpick inserted in the center comes out clean.

- Use 1 tablespoon pumpkin pie spice in place of the five separate spices.

PANNA COTTA

Panna cotta is Italian for "cooked cream." Though it looks fancy, it is very easy to make and is a wonderful summer dessert when topped with sweetened strawberries or lemon sauce.

Makes 6 servings

1 cup whipping cream
⅓ cup granulated sugar
1 (¼-ounce) envelope gelatin (about 1 tablespoon)
⅓ cup cold water
1½ cups buttermilk
2 teaspoons vanilla extract
1 teaspoon grated lemon zest
¼ teaspoon salt
Sugared strawberries or Lemon Sauce (page 183), for topping

Set out 6 small ramekins or custard cups.

Place the cream and sugar in a saucepan over medium-low heat, stirring until the sugar has dissolved. Remove from the heat. In a small bowl, sprinkle the gelatin over the water and stir with a fork until the gelatin has dissolved and the liquid is clear. Scrape all of the mixture out of the bowl and add it to the warm cream. Stir until the gelatin mixture is well incorporated.

Add the buttermilk, vanilla, lemon zest, and salt to the saucepan; stir thoroughly to combine. Rinse the ramekins or custard cups in cold water, then fill them with the custard mixture. Chill uncovered in the refrigerator just until cold, then cover with plastic wrap. Refrigerate for several hours or overnight.

At serving time, run a knife around the edges of the ramekins to loosen the panna cottas. Turn them out (upside down) onto dessert plates and top with some sugared sliced strawberries or lemon sauce before serving.

CRÈME BRÛLÉE

Your guests will never know that this version of the traditional eggy custard is eggless! Make in individual ramekins for a special-occasion dessert.

Makes 6 servings

1 (3.4-ounce) package vanilla instant pie and pudding mix
1½ cups whole milk
1¼ cups half-and-half
2 teaspoons vanilla extract
1 teaspoon finely grated orange zest
¼ cup light brown sugar

Set 6 individual ramekin dishes or custard cups on a baking sheet.

Whisk the pudding mix, milk, half-and-half, vanilla, and orange zest for 2 minutes by hand or with an electric mixer on medium speed. Immediately pour the mixture into the individual dishes. Let set for 5 minutes, then cover with clear plastic wrap and chill for at least 6 hours or overnight.

About 10 minutes before serving, preheat the broiler with a rack in the top broiling position. Remove the plastic wrap just as soon as the pudding is removed from the refrigerator so any droplets of condensation do not fall on the pudding. If any moisture is present, blot with a paper towel.

Sieve the sugar evenly and directly onto the top of the puddings just before placing them under the broiler. Broil for about 1½ minutes, or until the sugar melts and just begins to brown. Watch very closely so the sugar does not burn. Serve the ramekins immediately on small plates while the crème is still chilled and the topping is crisp.

VARIATION

GRAND MARNIER CRÈME BRÛLÉE: Omit the vanilla, reduce the milk by 2 tablespoons, and add ¼ cup Grand Marnier.

CRÊPES SUZETTE WITH ICE CREAM

Make the crêpes and the ice cream balls ahead of time, and this elegant and impressive dessert will be easy to assemble at the end of dinner.

Makes 6 servings

1 quart eggless Old-Fashioned Vanilla Ice Cream (page 188)
One recipe Dessert Crêpes (page 83)

ORANGE SAUCE

½ cup granulated sugar
1 tablespoon cornstarch
¾ cup cold water
2 tablespoons butter
3 tablespoons orange juice
Finely grated zest of ½ orange
⅛ teaspoon nutmeg

⅓ cup shredded sweetened coconut, for garnish

Make small balls (about ¼ cup each) of ice cream ahead of time and place them on a chilled tray. Return them to the freezer immediately. When they have frozen hard, store in a covered container in the freezer until ready to assemble the dessert.

ORANGE SAUCE: Place the sugar and cornstarch in a small saucepan. Stir to combine; add the water. Place over medium-high heat and stir as the mixture comes to a boil. Reduce the heat and continue stirring until the sauce becomes clear and thickened. Remove it from the heat and add the butter, orange juice and zest, and nutmeg. Stir to mix. Assemble dessert immediately or reheat sauce in the microwave for a few seconds to warm before serving.

To assemble the dessert, place a warmed crêpe on a dessert plate and put 2 scoops of ice cream on one side of the crêpe. Fold the top half over, then pour a generous spoonful of orange sauce over the crêpe. Sprinkle with a bit of shredded coconut. Serve immediately.

APPLE CRÊPES

These delicate crêpes, filled with buttery cinnamon apples,
make a lovely dessert or a special side dish for brunch.

Makes 6 servings

3 tablespoons butter
4 tart apples, peeled, cored, and cut into thin slices
⅓ cup granulated sugar
½ cup white wine or water
2 teaspoons ground cinnamon
2 teaspoons fresh lemon juice
One recipe Dessert Crêpes (page 83)
Eggless vanilla ice cream or sweetened whipped cream, for topping

Melt the butter in a sauté pan. Add the apple slices, stirring to coat them in butter. Add the sugar, wine or water, and cinnamon; continue cooking over medium heat until the apples are tender but still hold their shape. Drizzle with the lemon juice and transfer to a bowl. Set aside at room temperature.

At serving time, warm the crêpes and filling separately. Place a spoonful of filling in the center of each crêpe, spread it evenly, and roll it up. Place the filled crêpe on a dessert plate, seam side down. Top with a scoop of vanilla ice cream or whipped cream, then spoon a little of the juice from the apples over the crêpes and ice cream.

CHEESECAKE WITH BLUEBERRY TOPPING

This special-occasion dessert may be made ahead and frozen. Use a 9- or 10-inch store-bought graham cracker piecrust if you don't have time to make the cheesecake completely from scratch. My favorite topping is a warm blueberry sauce, but you can substitute sugared sliced strawberries, Lemon Sauce (page 183), or chocolate sauce.

Serves 8

CRUST

About 16 graham crackers (to make 1½ cups crumbs)
6 tablespoons (¾ stick) butter, melted
1 tablespoon granulated sugar

CHEESECAKE

1 (8-ounce) package full-fat cream cheese, at room temperature
1 (8-ounce) package low-fat cream cheese, at room temperature
½ cup granulated sugar
⅓ cup canned sweetened condensed milk
2 teaspoons fresh lemon juice
½ teaspoon finely grated lemon zest

2 teaspoons vanilla extract

2 tablespoons cornstarch

1½ teaspoons Ener-G Egg Replacer powder

¾ teaspoon baking powder

⅛ teaspoon baking soda

¾ cup low-fat sour cream

BLUEBERRY TOPPING

2 tablespoons granulated sugar

1 teaspoon cornstarch

1 tablespoon water

2 cups fresh or frozen blueberries

1 teaspoon fresh lemon juice

CRUST: Crush the graham crackers in a food processor until very fine (or place the crackers in a plastic bag and smash them with a rolling pin). Place the crumbs in a bowl. Stir in the butter and sugar with a fork, then press the mixture into the bottom and up the sides of a 9- or 10-inch pie pan. Chill uncovered for 1 hour before filling.

Preheat the oven to 300 degrees.

CHEESECAKE: Put the cream cheeses, sugar, condensed milk, lemon juice and zest, and vanilla in a medium bowl and beat with a handheld mixer until very smooth, scraping the sides of the bowl. Combine the cornstarch, egg replacer powder, baking powder, and baking soda in a small bowl and add them to the cream cheese mixture. Continue beating with the hand mixer until well blended, then beat in the sour cream.

Pour the mixture into the graham cracker crust and spread evenly. Place the cheese-cake on a cookie sheet and bake for 1 hour. Turn off the oven. Keep the cheesecake in the oven and leave the door ajar for another 2 hours; it will set up as it cools. Remove from the oven and cool to room temperature, then wrap tightly and refrigerate the cheesecake overnight so that it will become completely firm.

BLUEBERRY TOPPING: Place the sugar and cornstarch in a small saucepan and stir to combine. Add the water and stir to mix. Add the blueberries and cook over medium heat, stirring until the sauce is slightly thickened and the berries have softened. Add the lemon juice.

To serve, cut the cheesecake into wedges and serve with a spoonful of the warm blueberry sauce or your favorite topping.

LEMON PIE WITH MARSHMALLOW TOPPING

A meringue is traditionally made with whipped egg whites. My mother created this "maringue" by using melted marshmallows instead, hence the alternate spelling. This pie does not have the typical peaks on top—but it's still scrumptious!

Makes 6 servings

9-inch frozen pie shell

FILLING

1 cup granulated sugar
5 tablespoons cornstarch
¼ teaspoon salt
1¼ cups water
3 tablespoons butter
2 teaspoons grated lemon zest
½ cup fresh lemon juice
2 drops yellow food coloring (optional)

MARINGUE

14 eggless marshmallows (not mini marshmallows)
½ cup confectioners' sugar, sifted
2 tablespoons hot water

Preheat the oven to 375 degrees. Defrost the pie shell for 10 minutes and prick the surface of the crust with a fork so it will not bubble while being baked. Bake the pie shell for 12 to 15 minutes, or until lightly browned. After 5 minutes in the oven, prick again if any bubbles appear on the surface of the crust. Cool the crust before filling.

FILLING: Combine the sugar, cornstarch, and salt in a saucepan. Add the water, then stir until the cornstarch is dissolved. Place over medium-high heat and stir continuously until the mixture comes to a gentle boil. Reduce the heat and simmer gently for 2 minutes, continuing to stir until the filling is clear and thickened. Remove the pan from the heat and add the butter, lemon zest and juice, and food coloring. Stir well, incorporating the butter as it melts.

Cool for 5 minutes, then pour the filling into the baked pie shell. (The filling may not be made ahead of time, as it will set up and won't be pourable.) Allow the pie to cool to room temperature or, if using later, cover and refrigerate.

Preheat the broiler with a rack in the top broiling position.

MARINGUE: Place the marshmallows, sugar, and water in a 2-quart microwaveable container, as the marshmallows will expand. Microwave until most of the marshmallows are very puffy. Stir them a bit, then microwave again until they are melted and foamy. Immediately stir and then spread the topping over the lemon filling. Leave a good ¼ inch of space between the outer rim of the crust and the marshmallow topping, as it will spread when broiled.

Place the pie under the broiler for 1½ to 2 minutes, depending on the intensity of the broiler, and watch closely until the topping is very lightly browned. Remove the pie from the oven and cool to room temperature before serving.

COOK'S NOTE

- Do not cover the lemon filling with the marshmallow topping and run under the broiler more than 1 hour before serving, as the topping will become soft.

STEAMED CRANBERRY PUDDING WITH VANILLA SAUCE

The Pilgrims called cranberries "crane berries," as it was thought the flower and stem of the cranberry bush resembled the head and bill of the cranes that fed on cranberries in the New England marshes. This steamed pudding was Christmas dessert when I was growing up, and it is still a favorite even with my grandchildren today.

Makes 6 servings

PUDDING

1½ cups all-purpose flour
2 teaspoons baking soda
½ teaspoon baking powder
½ teaspoon cinnamon
½ teaspoon salt
2 cups cranberries, fresh or frozen (partially thawed after measuring)
½ cup molasses
⅓ cup hot water

VANILLA SAUCE

⅓ cup (5⅓ tablespoons) butter
1 cup unsifted confectioners' sugar
2 teaspoons all-purpose flour
⅔ cup cold water
1½ teaspoons vanilla extract

In a large pot fitted with a steaming rack, bring about 2 inches of water to an active simmer. Generously grease a lidded 5- to 6-cup steamed pudding mold that fits into the steamer.

PUDDING: Mix the flour, baking soda, baking powder, cinnamon, and salt in a medium bowl. Cut the cranberries in half with scissors or chop coarsely and gently combine them with the flour mixture. Stir in the molasses and water until just blended.

Spoon the batter into the prepared mold and smooth the top, filling it no more than two-thirds full. Cover the mold tightly. Place it in the steamer with the simmering water and steam for about 2½ hours. It is important that the water is continually moving but not actively boiling. Check occasionally to see that the water level isn't getting too low, adding more boiling water to replenish it as needed.

Unmold the pudding immediately onto a serving plate and slice it into serving pieces.

VANILLA SAUCE: In a small saucepan, melt the butter over low heat. Blend in the sugar and flour, then add the water and vanilla. Cook over medium-low heat, stirring occasionally until slightly thickened. The sauce may be made ahead of time and reheated slowly. Top each slice of pudding with a spoonful of the sauce.

COOK'S NOTES

- RING MOLDS: It is important to use a ring mold or a tube mold so the heat reaches the center of the pudding and cooks the berries. If you don't have a ring mold, you can create one by placing a small metal can in the center of the mold and filling the outer space with batter.

- MAKING A HOMEMADE STEAMER: Here are several ways to set up a steamer. 1) Place a round rack in the bottom of a large kettle; the rack should be at least ¾ inch up from the bottom of the kettle. Set the covered mold on top of the rack and pour boiling water into the kettle to reach 1 inch up the side of the mold. 2) Remove the tops, bottoms, and any paper wrappers from three short 5-ounce metal cans (like a tuna can). Place them in the bottom of a large stockpot with a lid and add water to the tops of the cans. Bring the water to a simmer and continue with the recipe. 3) Set a metal, fan-type vegetable steamer in a large stockpot. Add 2 inches of water, bring to a simmer, and continue with the recipe.

- MAKING A TIGHT-FITTING LID: A tight lid can be created by covering any heatproof mold with a double layer of foil and tying the edges down tightly with a string or a rubber band.

- INDIVIDUAL PUDDINGS: Preheat the oven to 325 degrees and generously grease 10 cupcake tins. Fill them just to the top and cover with a piece of lightly greased foil that is secure on the sides, but leaves space for the puddings to expand. Bake 30 to 35 minutes. Turn out onto a wire rack. To serve, place the warm puddings bottom side up on individual plates and top with vanilla sauce.

- HOLDING THE PUDDING: This pudding will hold nicely for an extra ½ hour in the steamer. Or the pudding may be steamed earlier in the day and unmolded. Cool to room temperature and wrap with plastic wrap until ready to reheat. At serving time, remove the plastic wrap and cover the whole pudding with a paper towel; warm it in a microwave on medium power. The pudding also freezes nicely.

STEAMED CHOCOLATE PUDDING

The original recipe for steamed chocolate pudding was from my mother's recipe file and it was always a favorite in our family. My eggless version is an excellent substitute, but make sure you follow the measurements and method exactly. It does take 2 hours to steam, but requires no last-minute work.

Makes 8 servings

2 ounces unsweetened chocolate
4 tablespoons (½ stick) butter
1 cup plus 3 tablespoons all-purpose flour
½ cup plus 1 tablespoon granulated sugar
2 teaspoons baking powder
¼ teaspoon salt
½ cup plus 2 tablespoons half-and-half
1 tablespoon Ener-G Egg Replacer, whisked with 2 tablespoons water until foamy
¾ teaspoon vanilla extract

Sweetened whipped cream or eggless vanilla ice cream, for topping

In a large pot fitted with a steaming rack, bring about 2 inches of water to an active simmer. Generously grease a covered 5- to 6-cup steamed pudding mold that fits into the steamer.

Melt the chocolate and butter in a small heatproof bowl over a pan of simmering water. Stir to blend with a fork or small whisk and cool slightly. Sift the flour, sugar, baking powder, and salt into a medium bowl. Add the half-and-half, egg replacer mixture, chocolate mixture, and vanilla to the flour mixture. (Use a rubber spatula to scrape out every bit of the egg replacer and chocolate from the small bowls.) Blend well using a rubber spatula or large spoon, stirring by hand until well mixed and all lumps are removed, but do not overbeat.

Spoon the batter into the prepared mold and smooth the top, filling it no more than two-thirds full. Cover the mold tightly. Place it in the steamer with the simmering water and steam for 2 hours, checking the water level occasionally and replenishing with more boiling water if needed.

Lift the mold from the steamer, remove the lid, and let rest at room temperature for 5 minutes before unmolding. Run a knife around the edge of the pudding and cover the mold with a serving plate. Invert and tap the mold to easily release the pudding. Cut into wedges and serve warm with sweetened whipped cream or a scoop of eggless vanilla ice cream.

COOK'S NOTES

- This pudding may be steamed earlier in the day, unmolded, cooled, and wrapped with plastic wrap. To reheat, remove the plastic wrap and cover the whole pudding with a paper towel; warm it in a microwave on medium power.

- See Steamed Cranberry Pudding with Vanilla Sauce (page 172) for additional instructions on cooking and equipment.

GRANDMOTHER'S RICE PUDDING

Warm, sweet, and soft, rice pudding is an ideal comfort food to take to friends. My mother made this family favorite often. It's versatile as well, lending itself to any number of substitutions and variations (see below).

Makes 6 servings

½ cup long-grain white rice
½ cup half-and-half
4 cups milk
½ cup granulated sugar
1½ teaspoons vanilla extract
Pinch of salt
1 tablespoon granulated sugar
1 teaspoon cinnamon

Combine the rice, half-and-half, milk, sugar, vanilla, and salt in the top of a double boiler and stir to blend. Cook uncovered over simmering water for 2 to 2½ hours, or until the rice is tender and the pudding has thickened. Stir the pudding every 20 minutes to prevent a film from forming on top of the milk.

To make the topping, stir the sugar and cinnamon together. When the rice is soft and the pudding is thick, pour it into a casserole dish or individual custard cups and sprinkle the cinnamon-and-sugar mixture evenly over the hot pudding. Run it under the broiler if a crisper topping is desired. Serve the pudding warm or at room temperature; however, refrigerate it if not serving within 1 hour.

VARIATIONS

BAKED RICE PUDDING: Preheat the oven to 325 degrees and grease a 2-quart oven-proof casserole dish. Combine the rice, half-and-half, milk, sugar, vanilla, and salt in the dish and stir to mix well. Place the uncovered dish in the oven and bake for 30 minutes. Stir and cover loosely with foil to prevent a crust from forming. Continue stirring every 30 minutes, for a total cooking time of 2½ hours. Remove the pudding from the oven when thickened slightly, stir to incorporate any film that has formed, and sprinkle with the combined sugar and cinnamon.

JASMINE RICE PUDDING: Substitute jasmine rice for the long-grain rice and add ½ cup raisins and 1 teaspoon grated lemon zest in place of the vanilla.

BROWN RICE PUDDING: Substitute long-grain brown rice for the white rice and add ½ cup chopped dates.

KEY LIME PIE

Key West, Florida, is the home of the Key lime pie, which became the state's official pie in 2006. In this version, cream cheese flavored with vanilla makes up for the lack of eggs. Key lime pie is traditionally made with Key limes, which are smaller and more tart than familiar green Persian limes. If you're pressed for time, feel free to use a 9- or 10-inch store-bought graham cracker piecrust.

Makes 6 servings

CRUST

1¼ cups graham cracker crumbs (from about 10 crackers)
6 tablespoons (¾ stick) butter, melted
1 tablespoon granulated sugar

FILLING

8 ounces cream cheese, softened
1 (14-ounce) can sweetened condensed milk, divided
2½ teaspoons finely grated Key lime zest
½ cup fresh Key lime juice (from 10 to 12 Key limes)
1 teaspoon vanilla extract

TOPPING

1 cup low-fat sour cream
¼ cup sifted confectioners' sugar
1 teaspoon vanilla extract
8 thin Key lime slices, for garnish

Preheat the oven to 350 degrees.

CRUST: Crush the graham crackers in a food processor until very fine (or place the crackers in a plastic bag and smash them with a rolling pin). Place the crumbs in a bowl. Stir in the butter and sugar with a fork, then press the mixture into the bottom and up the sides of a 9-inch pie pan. Bake the crust for about 8 minutes, or until slightly darkened and set. Cool the crust before filling.

FILLING: Place the cream cheese and half the condensed milk in a medium bowl. Beat with a handheld electric beater until smooth. Add the remaining condensed milk, lime zest and juice, and vanilla. Beat until very smooth. Pour into the cooled crust; cover and chill for 1 hour or overnight.

TOPPING: Beat the sour cream, sugar, and vanilla together with an electric beater until light and fluffy.

Serve each piece of pie with a spoonful of topping and garnish with a lime slice.

APPLE GALETTE

A fruit galette, as the term has evolved in American cuisine, refers to an open-faced, free-form fruit tart with the crust ruffling up around its border. This recipe makes two delicious apple galettes— one to serve and one to freeze! The secret to this recipe is the mouthwatering apple syrup that is poured over the finished pie.

Makes 2 medium galettes, 5 to 6 servings each

3½ pounds crisp cooking apples
¾ cup granulated sugar, divided

1 (14.1-ounce) package Pillsbury Piecrusts (2 crusts) or a double batch of Basic
    Piecrust (page 182)
2 teaspoons all-purpose flour
½ teaspoon cinnamon
1 teaspoon finely grated lemon zest
2 tablespoons fresh lemon juice

Peel, core, and slice the apples into ⅓-inch slices; place in a large bowl. Sprinkle ½ cup of the sugar over the apples and stir to coat slices. Set the apples aside for 30 minutes, stirring twice or so.

Preheat the oven to 425 degrees.

Unroll the two premade or homemade crusts onto separate pieces of plastic wrap, dust each side with flour, and cover them with an additional sheet of plastic wrap. Using a rolling pin, roll each crust out to 12 inches in diameter.

Line two baking sheets with parchment paper or foil that has been sprayed with cooking oil and transfer each crust to a baking sheet.

Using a large, slotted spoon, transfer the apple slices to a second bowl, reserving all of the juice that has collected in the bottom of the first bowl. Pour this juice into a small saucepan and set aside.

Combine the flour, the remaining ¼ cup sugar, and cinnamon in a small bowl. Sprinkle it, along with the lemon zest and juice over the apples. Stir well to combine, and divide the apples between the two crusts, arranging them in an even layer in the center and leaving a 2-inch margin of crust around the apples. Fold the crust partly up the sides of the apples and crimp or fold it as needed to make a nice round shape. Leave 4 to 5 inches of the center uncovered. Note: if you feel confident enough to move the two now-smaller galettes to one baking sheet to bake, do that here.

Bake for 10 minutes, then lower the temperature to 375 degrees. Bake for 30 to 40 minutes more, or until the juices are bubbling and the apples are tender when pierced with a fork and the crust is light brown.

While the galettes are baking, place the saucepan with the reserved apple juice over medium-high heat and bring to a boil. Reduce the heat, stir, and continue to simmer until the sauce is slightly thickened like light syrup. Immediately remove from the heat so you don't over-reduce the syrup.

When the galettes are done, remove the baking sheets from the oven and place them on 2 wire racks. Pour the warm syrup over the apples, dividing it between the two galettes and scraping the saucepan with a rubber spatula to get all the syrup out. When the galettes have cooled for 10 minutes, remove them from the baking sheets with two wide metal spatulas and transfer them to a large serving plate, before any juices caramelize beneath the crust. Serve warm or at room temperature.

BLUEBERRY SQUARES

Whenever I make this dish, people clamor for the recipe. The finished servings look like a square sandwich with blueberry sauce and whipped cream for a filling, and the top crust is dusted with confectioners' sugar. The filling and crust may be prepared ahead of time, or even frozen, then assembled quickly at serving time.

Serves 9

CRUST

2 cups all-purpose flour
1 cup (2 sticks) cold butter
¼ cup ice-cold water

FILLING

1 cup plus 1 tablespoon granulated sugar, divided
2 tablespoons cornstarch
½ cup water
3 cups blueberries, fresh or frozen
1 tablespoon fresh lemon juice
1 cup whipping cream
½ teaspoon vanilla extract
½ cup confectioners' sugar, for dusting

Preheat the oven to 300 degrees. Have ready two ungreased baking sheets.

CRUST: Place the flour in a medium bowl and cut in butter with two knives or a pastry blender. Stir in the water with a fork and gather the dough into two equal-size balls. Do not overwork the pastry.

Roll each piece of dough into a 10-inch square (do your best to shape the dough while rolling it, then trim the edges with a knife to form square sides) and place each on a baking sheet. Prick the surface well with a fork before placing the crust in the oven. Bake for 1¼ hours, switching the position of the sheets in the oven after 45 minutes. With a long, sharp knife, cut each crust into 9 equal squares while still hot, then cool them on the baking sheets. These may be stored in an airtight container for several days or frozen.

FILLING: Combine 1 cup of the sugar and the cornstarch in a medium saucepan. Stir in the water and berries. Cook over medium heat, stirring, until the sauce is glossy and thickened. Remove from the heat and stir in the lemon juice.

To assemble, whip the cream to soft peaks, adding the remaining 1 tablespoon sugar and vanilla any time after you have started beating.

Place one pastry square on each dessert plate. Top with a large spoonful of berry filling, then a spoonful of whipped cream. Place a second square of pastry on top and lightly dust it with confectioners' sugar just before serving.

COOK'S NOTE

- Eggless vanilla ice cream may be substituted for the whipped cream.

APPLE TWISTS WITH CINNAMON SAUCE

Premade piecrust makes this dessert easy, but the flavor—old-fashioned apple pie—is anything but store bought.

Makes 8 servings

1 (14.1-ounce) package Pillsbury Piecrusts, or 1 recipe Basic Piecrust (recipe follows)

2 large tart cooking apples, peeled, cored, and cut into 8 wedges

6 tablespoons (¾ stick) butter, melted

½ cup granulated sugar

1½ teaspoons cinnamon

¾ cup water

Eggless vanilla ice cream, for topping

Preheat the oven to 450 degrees. Lightly grease a 9-by-13-inch baking pan.

On a lightly floured surface, roll the packaged or homemade piecrust into a rectangle about 10 by 16 inches. Starting in the middle of the rectangle, cut the rolled pastry into 1-by-10-inch strips. Wrap one strip around each apple wedge in a spiral, covering the wedge; place the loose end down in the prepared pan. Brush with the butter.

Combine the sugar and cinnamon and sprinkle on top of the apple twists. Pour the water around the pastry rolls (not on top of them) and immediately put the pan into the oven. Bake for 25 to 30 minutes, or until lightly browned.

Serve two warm pieces on each plate with a scoop of vanilla ice cream as a topping; spoon any leftover sauce from the baking dish over the ice cream.

BASIC PIECRUST

*Homemade piecrust adds wonderful flavor and crispness to
pies and tarts. If you are making a double-crust pie, simply
double this recipe. Sprinkle any small bits of leftover crust
that don't make it onto your pie with cinnamon and sugar,
then bake at 375 degrees for 10 to 12 minutes, until the pieces
are very lightly browned. These sweet morsels are a great
snack for kids who can't wait for the real pie to be finished.*

Makes 1 pie shell to fit a 10-inch pie pan

1½ cups all-purpose flour

½ teaspoon salt

½ cup (1 stick) cold butter, cut into chunks

2 tablespoons shortening
4 to 5 tablespoons ice water

Place the flour and salt in a bowl. Using two knives or a pastry blender, cut the butter and shortening into the flour until crumbly. Add the water and mix lightly with a fork to form a ball of dough that is not sticky. Do not overwork the dough by trying to include all the last bits of flour. Flatten the ball into a thick disk, wrap it in plastic wrap, and chill for about 30 minutes before rolling out—especially if the kitchen is warm. (The dough may also be made the day before, wrapped, and chilled. Before rolling, allow the dough to warm at room temperature for 20 to 30 minutes.)

Get out your 10-inch pie pan. Roll the dough on a lightly floured board until 1 inch larger around the edge than the pie pan. Roll the dough up on the rolling pin and then unroll it over the pie pan. Gently pat the dough down so it fits snugly into the sides of the pan. Trim the excess dough around the edge, leaving about 1 inch beyond the edge of the pan. Crimp the edges decoratively.

Follow your chosen recipe for specifics on filling or prebaking the piecrust.

COOK'S NOTE

*   If you double the recipe, you can have a second piecrust to freeze. Lay the second piece of rolled dough between two layers of plastic wrap and roll it up like a scroll. Wrap well and freeze, thaw in the refrigerator, and bake as needed.

LEMON SAUCE

*This sauce is lovely over unfrosted cake,
panna cotta, or fresh blueberries.*

Makes 1½ cups

½ cup granulated sugar
1 tablespoon cornstarch
⅛ teaspoon salt
1 cup boiling water

2 tablespoons butter
1 tablespoon grated lemon zest
3 tablespoons fresh lemon juice

Blend the sugar, cornstarch, and salt in a small saucepan. Place over medium heat and slowly add the hot water, stirring until the sauce begins to thicken. Add the butter and continue stirring until the sauce is clear and thickens more. Remove it from the heat and stir in the lemon zest and juice. The sauce may be covered and stored in the refrigerator for 2 days and reheated over low heat.

FROZEN DESSERTS

TIPS AND HINTS

- **Shopping for Eggless Ice Cream:** A number of good eggless ice creams and sorbets are available at the market; however, in some cases it may take a little shopping and comparing to find the brand you prefer. Sorbet is a good alternative for eggless folks, since it should not contain eggs but still has the cold sweetness of ice cream. As always, read the label each time you buy a container (even sorbet) as the ingredients may change from time to time.

- **Methods for Homemade Ice Cream:** Even though store-bought ice cream works in a pinch, I find that making my own yields a much better flavor, and it's really not that difficult. The following two methods for making eggless ice cream or sorbet at home work equally well.

  » **Freezer Method**: Have all your ingredients well mixed and at room temperature or slightly cooled before pouring them into an open cake pan or other similar container. Place on the shelf in the freezer for at least 2 hours, or until just frozen. Meanwhile, chill the bowl of a food processor in the refrigerator. Break up the frozen ice cream or sorbet and scrape it into the food processor bowl; pulse just until it becomes smooth, but do not allow the mixture to become liquid. (Alternatively, you can chill a mixing bowl and use a handheld mixer to smooth out the frozen ice cream chunks.) Place the ice cream or sorbet in a prechilled freezer-safe container, cover, and freeze it for several hours or until serving time.

  » **Ice-Cream Maker Method**: Have all the ingredients mixed together and well chilled before pouring them into an ice-cream maker. Follow the manufacturer's directions. For best results, fill the ice-cream maker no more than two-thirds full. When the freezing process is complete, serve or immediately spoon the ice cream into a prechilled, freezer-safe container. Cover and place in the freezer.

- **Preparing the Fruit or Flavoring:** Prepare the fruit or flavoring *before* making the basic vanilla ice cream recipe. Chill it well before adding it to the ice cream base.

- **Sweetening Ice Cream and Sorbet**: Ice creams and sorbets will always taste a little less sweet when frozen, so taste them before freezing; the liquid base should be a little sweeter than you want the finished product to be.

- **Egg Alert**: Some frozen yogurt contains egg. Always check the labels.

OLD-FASHIONED VANILLA ICE CREAM

*My friend Janet knows about my allergy to eggs, so she
made this ice cream and served it at her recent anniversary
celebration. She was kind enough to share the recipe with
me. It has a wonderful, old-fashioned creamy texture that
takes me back to the days of hand-churned ice cream,
where the mixture was placed in a covered container
and packed in ice chips and salt to finish freezing.*

Makes 2 quarts

1 cup whole milk
¾ cup plus 2 tablespoons sugar
¼ teaspoon salt
1 cup half-and-half
1 tablespoon vanilla extract
2 cups whipping cream

Scald the milk by heating it in a medium saucepan until bubbles just begin to form
around the edge of the pan. Immediately remove from the heat and add the sugar
and salt. Stir until dissolved. Cover and refrigerate for 30 minutes or longer. Add the
half-and-half, vanilla, and whipping cream to the milk mixture. Stir to combine, then
pour the mixture into an ice-cream maker and freeze as directed—or use the Freezer
Method on page 186.

VARIATIONS

STRAWBERRY ICE CREAM: Omit the vanilla and add 2 cups of chilled, pureed strawberries to the mixture before freezing.

PEACH ICE CREAM: Omit the vanilla and add 2 cups of chilled, coarsely pureed
peaches to the mixture before freezing.

MINT–CHOCOLATE CHIP ICE CREAM: Omit the vanilla and add 1 teaspoon peppermint extract, ¼ teaspoon green food coloring, and 1 cup chocolate chips to the mixture before freezing.

COOK'S NOTE

- Because the sweetness level of fresh fruits is unpredictable, taste the ice cream base after adding the fruit but before chilling, as extra sugar may need to be added.

LIGHT VANILLA ICE CREAM

This version of a light ice cream has a gelatin base and omits the heavy cream. It makes a wonderful base for fruit and chocolate ice creams.

Makes 1¼ quarts

1 (0.25-ounce) envelope unflavored gelatin
2 tablespoons cold water
2 cups milk
¾ cup sugar
¼ teaspoon salt
2 cups half-and-half
2½ teaspoons vanilla extract

Prefreeze an ice-cream maker bowl. Soften the gelatin in the water according to package directions. Scald the milk by heating it in a medium saucepan until bubbles just begin to form around the edge of the pan. Immediately remove the pan from the heat. Dissolve the gelatin mixture in the milk and add the sugar and salt. Stir to mix well. Cool in the refrigerator for no longer than 30 minutes, stirring two or three times. Do not overchill, as the gelatin will begin to set up.

Add the half-and-half and vanilla to the gelatin mixture. Stir well and pour into the ice-cream maker; freeze as directed or use the Freezer Method on page 186.

VARIATIONS

TROPICAL TREAT ICE CREAM: Combine 3 mashed bananas, 1 cup mashed strawberries, and ¼ cup additional sugar. Combine and chill for 1 hour before adding to the vanilla ice cream base. Stir well and freeze in two batches.

TOFFEE TREAT ICE CREAM: Stir in 1 cup crushed toffee-flavored hard candy pieces to the ice cream mixture before freezing.

PEACHY PLUS ICE CREAM: Place 4 chopped fresh or thawed frozen peaches and ½ cup additional sugar in a bowl and stir to mix well. Chill thoroughly before adding to the ice cream base. Stir well and freeze in two batches, since one batch may be too large for some home ice-cream makers.

CHOCOLATE–CHOCOLATE CHIP ICE CREAM: Add ½ cup chocolate syrup and 1 cup semisweet chocolate mini-morsels to the ice cream base.

PEACH ICE CREAM

Ripe summer peaches are so juicy and they add so much flavor to ice cream. Raspberries tossed with a bit of sugar make a colorful topping for this refreshing summer dessert—my favorite!

Makes 1½ pints

1½ cups milk
½ cup light corn syrup
2 large peaches, peeled and sliced
¼ cup granulated sugar
¼ cup orange juice
1 tablespoon fresh lemon juice
½ teaspoon grated lemon zest
½ teaspoon vanilla extract

Scald the milk by heating it in a medium saucepan until bubbles just begin to form around the edge of the pan. Immediately remove the pan from the heat and pour it into a heatproof bowl. Add the corn syrup, then stir until well mixed; cool to room temperature. Mash the peaches and sugar together with a potato masher or blender, retaining some small lumps of fruit. Add the peach mixture to the cooled milk along with the orange juice, lemon juice and zest, and vanilla. Stir well and chill for 1 to 2 hours.

Pour the mixture into an ice-cream maker and freeze as directed. Alternatively, use the Freezer Method on page 186.

LEMON SORBET PIE

While I love lemon sorbet, this pie can be made with any flavor of sorbet, ice cream, or frozen yogurt. The spiced crumb crust adds interest to this easy dessert. Be creative!

Makes 6 servings

CRUMBS

¾ cup fine crumbs made from leftover yellow cake or vanilla cookies
½ cup brown sugar
1 teaspoon cinnamon
½ teaspoon nutmeg
¼ teaspoon ground cloves
¼ teaspoon ground ginger
3 tablespoons butter, melted

FILLING

1 tablespoon grated lemon zest
1 pint lemon sorbet, softened slightly
Raspberries or strawberries, for garnish

CRUMBS: Preheat the oven to 325 degrees. Place the cake or cookie crumbs into a pie pan and place into the oven. Bake cake crumbs for 15 minutes; bake cookie crumbs for 10 minutes. Stir every 5 minutes. Remove the pie pan from the oven when the crumbs begin to darken. Immediately spoon the crumbs into a bowl to cool and prevent over-browning. Add the sugar, cinnamon, nutmeg, cloves, and ginger and stir to combine. Stir the butter into the crumbs with a fork. Press the crumb mixture firmly into an 8-inch pie pan, covering the bottom and sides of the pan. Place in the freezer for 30 minutes.

FILLING: Remove the crust from the freezer. Stir the lemon zest into the sorbet and spread into the crust. Cover the pie with plastic wrap and immediately return to the freezer for at least 3 hours.

To serve, place the pie in the refrigerator for 20 minutes before serving to slightly soften it before cutting. Cut it into 6 wedges and garnish each serving with a few berries.

ICE CREAM PARFAITS

You can prepare this fun dessert well ahead of time and store it in the freezer. To really show off the layers, I love to make the parfaits in glass coffee mugs or clear plastic cups (the latter for more casual occasions). If you have access to old-fashioned parfait glasses, even better! Filling a tray with parfaits and passing them around in a crowd always garners oohs and aahs.

Eggless vanilla ice cream (or your flavor of choice)
Berry jam, chocolate syrup, fresh sugared sliced strawberries, or a thickened fruit
    sauce
Sweetened whipped cream or dessert topping (optional)
Crushed Oreos or crumbled eggless sugar cookies (optional)

Chill the number of parfait glasses or cups you'd like to serve in the freezer at least 15 minutes before filling.

Put a large scoop or spoonful of ice cream in each glass, top with a scant tablespoon of jam, syrup, strawberries, or sauce, then cover with another large scoop of ice cream. You may press the ice cream slightly to compress it, but do not try to make perfect layers—these parfaits are meant to look rustic. Alternate the ice cream with your layering ingredient of choice until the glass is almost filled or the parfait is the size you want to serve. End with a spoonful of your layering ingredient of choice.

Cover the glasses with plastic wrap and immediately put them on a tray in the freezer. If desired, top each parfait with a spoonful of whipped cream or cookie crumbs at serving time.

LEMON YOGURT ICE CREAM

Top this tangy and refreshing ice cream with raspberry sauce for a colorful finish to a summer meal.

Makes 1 generous quart

4 cups (1 quart) low-fat or nonfat plain yogurt
1 teaspoon grated lemon zest
⅔ cup frozen lemonade concentrate, slightly thawed

Combine the yogurt, lemon zest, and lemonade concentrate in a medium bowl. Mix thoroughly and chill. Pour the mixture into an ice-cream maker and process as directed, or use the Freezer Method on page 186.

BRANDY ICE

This is a festive ending to an adults-only dinner and so easy to make. You can substitute different liqueurs, if you like. I love to serve a plate of small chocolate cookies alongside the ice. Plan ahead, as this dessert must be made at least 24 hours in advance.

Makes 8 servings

2 quarts eggless vanilla ice cream (not vanilla ice milk)
⅓ cup Cointreau
⅓ cup apricot brandy
⅓ cup Kahlúa

Prechill a freezer container. Soften the ice cream in the refrigerator just enough so the liqueurs can be stirred in (but do not let the ice cream completely melt). Stir in the liqueurs by hand or use an electric hand mixer on low speed (don't use a food processor or blender). Pour the mixture into the prechilled container and cover tightly.

Freeze for 24 hours before serving. Because of the alcohol, this dessert will not freeze solid, but it will keep well in the freezer like regular ice cream.

Spoon the ice into eight goblets or glass mugs and serve each with a small spoon.

FROZEN RUM-MOCHA CRÉME

Chocolate chips are the perfect sweet foil to this coffee- and rum-flavored ice cream. It's one of my favorite ways to conclude dinner with friends.

Makes 6 servings

1 quart eggless vanilla ice cream
¼ cup light rum
¼ cup dark rum
¼ cup Kahlúa
2 teaspoons instant coffee granules
⅓ cup miniature chocolate chips, or ⅓ cup chopped chocolate

Chill a food processor bowl and metal blade in the freezer for 1 hour, along with six large wine glasses or glass coffee mugs.

Combine the ice cream, rums, Kahlúa, and coffee granules in the food processor bowl. (You may also use a handheld electric mixer or stiff wire whisk, after the ice cream has softened a little, to combine the ingredients.) Blend until just mixed, then pour into the chilled glasses or mugs.

Freeze for several hours; note that the ice cream will not freeze solid because of the liqueur. Top with some chocolate chips or chopped chocolate and serve.

EGGLESS EGGNOG

If you thought you could never enjoy this rich holiday treat, think again. Cheers! Plan ahead as the eggnog mixture needs to chill at least 1½ hours before serving.

Serves 6 to 8

1 (3.4-ounce) packet vanilla instant pudding and pie mix
1 cup whole milk
¾ cup half-and-half
1 cup whipping cream, divided
4 teaspoons granulated sugar
¼ teaspoon salt
½ cup bourbon
2½ tablespoons rum
Fresh nutmeg, for grating

In a medium bowl, place the pudding mix, milk, half-and-half, ½ cup of the whipping cream, sugar, and salt. Whisk for 1 minute. Cover the mixture and chill it in the refrigerator for at least 1 hour and up to 4 hours, whisking once after the first ½ hour to again thoroughly blend the ingredients.

Whip the remaining ½ cup of whipping cream in a small bowl using a hand mixer until soft peaks form. Remove the pudding mixture from the refrigerator and stir in the bourbon and rum, then fold in the whipped cream. Cover and chill for at least 30 minutes.

To serve, pour the eggnog into punch cups and top with a grating of nutmeg.

COOK'S NOTE

*   To make a nonalcoholic version, omit the bourbon and rum, and add 1 teaspoon rum flavoring or vanilla extract and ¼ teaspoon cinnamon to the milk mixture.

MENUS AND PARTY IDEAS FOR KIDS AND FAMILIES

TIPS AND HINTS

- **Preparing Food**: Allowing kids to help prepare their favorite eggless dishes will enable them to better understand their food allergy and how different ingredients are used.

- **Checking Ingredients**: When children are young, have them help check the ingredients listed on packaged foods while you are grocery shopping together. Starting early will ensure that this checking is second nature to them as they get older. It will also help young people feel they're in control of their food choices and of their health.

- **Healthy Habits**: Children with food allergies who are exposed to good food habits early in life and are taught to have a watchful eye over their food preparation will find that dealing with food allergies early on will make it second nature as they grow up.

- **Planning**: Children (and teens, particularly) want foods that their friends like to eat, so include them in the planning. Inviting their best friend to work with you in the kitchen is a great idea as well. They'll probably come up with ideas for recipes you hadn't thought of!

- **Stocking Up**: Keep individual portions of your kid's favorite foods and casseroles, including cake squares, in the freezer for last-minute occasions.

CARNIVAL TIME BIRTHDAY PARTY

Use bright primary colors for paper tablecloths, napkins, and plates. Set out games suitable for the children's ages and have a contest to see who can name the most circus animals. Active kids like food that is easy and quick to eat.

Cornbread Hot Dog Bites (recipe follows)
Fried or roasted chicken
Carrot sticks and chips with Santa Fe Dip (recipe follows)
Apple wedges dipped in caramel sauce
Oatmeal Cookies (page 124)
Variety of juice boxes
Striped candy sticks

CORNBREAD HOT DOG BITES

Makes 18 pieces

1 (8.5-ounce) package Jiffy Corn Muffin Mix
¾ teaspoon xanthan gum
½ cup milk
2 teaspoons vegetable oil
6 hot dogs, cut into 1-inch pieces
Ketchup and mustard, for serving

Preheat the oven to 375 degrees. Place paper liners in mini muffin tins and spray them generously with cooking spray.

In a medium bowl, stir the corn muffin mix and xanthan gum together. Add the milk and oil. Stir until well mixed and spoon into the prepared muffin tins, filling to two-thirds full. Press one piece of hot dog into the center of each muffin batter.

Bake for 10 to 12 minutes, or until the cornbread begins to brown slightly on the edges. Remove the bites immediately from the pan and cool on a wire rack. Serve hot with ketchup and mustard for dipping.

SANTA FE DIP

Makes about 1 cup

2 tablespoons dry taco seasoning mix (half of one 1.25-ounce package)
½ cup eggless mayonnaise
½ cup low-fat sour cream

Stir the taco mix, mayonnaise, and sour cream together in a small bowl. Cover and chill for 1 hour to blend the flavors.

GAMES AND ACTIVITIES

Can Toss: Spray-paint six large coffee cans in bright colors and place them on the floor a short distance away. Let each child try and toss three small stuffed animals into the cans. Winners get to keep the animals.

End the party with a colorful animal piñata.

KIDS' STORYBOOK SLEEPOVER

Sleepovers are always fun. Have guests bring their favorite book so the kids can share the stories with each other.

EVENING SNACKS

Carrot sticks and chips with Yogurt Dip (recipe follows)
Raspberry Crystal Cups (recipe follows)
Refrigerator Sugar Cookies (page 128)

BREAKFAST TIME!

Orange juice and milk
Fruit Skewers (recipe follows)
Buttermilk Pancakes with Blueberries (page 44) with Extras (suggestions follow)
Syrup

YOGURT DIP

Makes 1¼ cups

½ cup plain Greek yogurt
½ cup eggless mayonnaise
1 tablespoon minced green onion (including green portion)
1 tablespoon minced sweet pickle
1 tablespoon minced parsley
1 teaspoon fresh lemon juice
1 teaspoon Dijon mustard
¼ teaspoon garlic salt

Combine all the ingredients in a small bowl and whisk together until blended. Cover and chill for 1 hour to blend the flavors.

RASPBERRY CRYSTAL CUPS

*Make these ahead and serve them in transparent cups. The
young and not-so-young alike love this light dessert.*

Serves 4

1 (3-ounce) package raspberry Jell-O
1 cup boiling water
1 cup minus 1 tablespoon cold water
1 tablespoon fresh lemon juice
1 cup fresh raspberries

Put the Jell-O powder into a medium bowl and add the boiling water, stirring until the gelatin is dissolved. Add the cold water and lemon juice. Cool to room temperature. Divide the raspberries between 4 glasses or clear cups and pour equal amounts of the gelatin mixture over the berries. Chill for several hours until firm.

FRUIT SKEWERS

Makes 8 skewers

3 fruits, such as strawberries, pineapple, large grapes, apples, mango, or bananas
2 tablespoons honey
2 tablespoons orange juice

Preheat the oven to 350 degrees. Soak eight 6-inch bamboo skewers in water for thirty minutes.

Cut the fruit into 1-inch chunks and thread alternating fruits of choice onto the skewers. Place onto a greased baking sheet. Combine the honey and orange juice in a small bowl and brush the mixture on the fruit skewers. Bake for 10 minutes, or until the fruit is lightly browned. Serve warm or at room temperature.

BUTTERMILK PANCAKE EXTRAS

Have small bowls of sliced bananas, raisins, chocolate chips, or blueberries ready so your guests' choice can be sprinkled on the uncooked side of the pancakes before turning.

HOLLYWOOD BIRTHDAY PARTY

Parties are an essential part of a teenager's life, and this one would suit a young teenager or a "tween" beautifully. For this Hollywood-themed bash, roll out a red paper carpet at the entry, rent a movie for after the meal, and give each guest a white bag of popcorn with their age in numerals in big red numbers. Set the food out on a table with plenty of napkins and extra plates, as the teens will keep coming back for more.

Apple Fizzies (recipe follows)
Assorted vegetable sticks with Yogurt Dip (page 200)
Baked Chicken Strips (page 118) with Honey-Mustard Sauce (page 101)
Yellow Cake with Raspberry Filling (page 148) (see decorating ideas that follow)
Old-Fashioned Vanilla Ice Cream (page 188), with chocolate sauce

APPLE FIZZIES

Serves 6 to 8

2 quarts apple juice
1 quart sparkling water or lemon soda
Ice cubes
1 lemon

In a large container, combine the apple juice, sparkling water or lemon soda, and ice cubes. Squeeze the juice from one-half of the lemon (about 2 tablespoons) and add it to the container. Stir well and pour into decorative glasses. Cut the remaining one-half lemon into wedges and perch them on the rims of the glasses before serving.

CAKE DECORATING IDEAS

Decorate a cake with fresh berries for a glamorous centerpiece. Place alternating fresh raspberries and blueberries in a spiral atop the frosting. Insert candles between the circles and place a fresh flower in the middle of the spiral. Space blueberries around the base of the frosted cake to mimic rows of theater lights.

Use a package of eggless marshmallows dipped in chocolate to decorate a show-stopping cake. Melt 8 ounces of semisweet chocolate in a double boiler. Using as many marshmallows as years to be celebrated, place a toothpick in each marshmallow and dip completely into the chocolate, then place them on the top of the cake and remove the toothpicks. Push the candles into the chocolate-coated marshmallows right away.

SOCCER GAME CELEBRATION

*Have everything ready when the hungry soccer players
come in the door! Win or lose, this meal will be a hit.
Use paper plates and napkins in the team's colors and
hang up a poster of a well-known soccer player. Let each
player tell about their best moment in the game.*

Popcorn with Corn Chips (recipe follows)
Water bottles with black-and-white striped labels
Chocolate milk and root beer
Cheeseburgers with Toppings (recipe follows)
Old-Fashioned Potato Salad (page 55)
Old-Fashioned Chocolate Chip Cookies (page 123)

Peeled oranges

POPCORN WITH CORN CHIPS

Serves 12

16 cups hot popped popcorn
4 cups corn chips
4 tablespoons (½ stick) butter or margarine, melted
1 (1-ounce) envelope ranch dressing mix
1 teaspoon garlic powder

Toss the popcorn and corn chips together in a large bowl. Stir together the butter or margarine, ranch dressing mix, and garlic powder until well mixed. Drizzle the mixture over the popcorn and chips, tossing quickly with a large spoon so the butter is evenly distributed.

CHEESEBURGERS WITH TOPPINGS

For each burger have the following ready:

Meat patty and bun
Square slice of cheese
Slices of tomato, onion, pickle, and lettuce
Eggless mayonnaise, ketchup, relish, and mustard

Just before the team arrives, cook the patties on a barbecue grill or in a frying pan. Place the toppings on platters and in bowls so the kids can help themselves.

AFTERNOON DOLL TEA PARTY

This party is perfect for young kids. Let them help prepare the party treats before they dress up their dolls for the afternoon tea. Be sure to prepare the food in small portions, as the children will want to pretend to feed their dolls. Decorate the table with a small bouquet of garden flowers and have a second plate, napkin, and spoon for each doll. Have the kids bring several changes of clothes for their dolls so they can put on a little play together with their dolls after the tea.

Cinnamon Toasts (recipe follows)
Sparkling Fruit Cups (recipe follows)
Brownies with Chocolate Frosting (page 142), Whipped Shortbread (page 135), and
    Raspberry Bars (page 138)

CINNAMON TOASTS

Have an assortment of different-shaped small cookie cutters on hand; the guests will love to choose their own and will have fun cutting their different shapes.

Makes 18 pieces

2½ tablespoons butter, softened
⅓ cup granulated sugar
½ teaspoon cinnamon
¼ teaspoon vanilla extract
6 slices white sandwich bread

Preheat the oven to 375 degrees. Grease a baking sheet or line it with parchment paper.

Combine the butter, sugar, cinnamon, and vanilla in a small bowl. Mix well and spread on one side of each bread slice. Have the guests cut the bread into different shapes using small cookie cutters to make three toasts from each slice. Place on a cookie sheet and bake for 8 to10 minutes, or until slightly crisp and just beginning to brown.

SPARKLING FRUIT CUPS

Sparkling lemon Jell-O with fruit is most refreshing and easy for children to manage with their dolls. Make the gelatin cups at least 3 hours ahead so they can set up and chill before serving.

Serves 8

1 (3-ounce) package lemon Jell-O
1 (13-ounce) can pineapple tidbits in light syrup (do not use fresh pineapple)
¾ cup plus 2 tablespoons sparkling water
1 (13-ounce) can mandarin oranges, well drained
1 cup whole green grapes, cut in half
Raspberries and halved strawberries, for garnish

Put the Jell-O in a medium bowl. Drain the juice from the pineapple tidbits (setting the tidbits aside) into a measuring cup and fill with water to make 1 cup. Pour the mixture into a saucepan and bring it to a boil. Pour the boiling liquid into the Jell-O, stirring until dissolved. Add the sparkling water and cool the mixture to room temperature.

Divide the pineapple bits, oranges, and grapes evenly between eight small clear plastic cups, then pour the Jell-O mixture over the fruit. Stir and chill until set (ideally at least 3 hours). Serve each cup topped with a couple of berries.

DR. SEUSS PLAYDATE PARTY FOR BUSY PRESCHOOLERS AND THEIR PARENTS

Invite a few parents and their preschoolers over for a morning of play. After reading The Lorax *(or another favorite Dr. Seuss book) to the preschoolers, bring out one picture for each child of the Lorax (or another character) along with some paper and crayons. Invite everyone to color his or her own version of the character. Put the drawings up on the wall and serve lunch. These treats are all portable—great for active kids with little hands!*

Serves 3 to 5 preschoolers and 3 adults

Sandwich quarters: Ham and cheese with eggless mayonnaise; peanut butter and jelly; and pesto, hummus, and avocado (recipes follow)
Watermelon Cups (recipe follows)
Cupcake Cones (recipe follows)

SANDWICHES

Ham and Cheese

6 slices whole wheat bread
3 slices ham
3 slices American cheese
3 tablespoons eggless mayonnaise
3 lettuce leaves

Assemble the sandwiches to each child's liking. Cut each sandwich into quarters and place on individual plates.

Peanut Butter and Jelly

6 slices of your child's favorite bread
Peanut butter
Jelly

Assemble the sandwiches and cut into quarters, then place onto a serving plate.

Hummus, Pesto, and Avocado

4 slices whole wheat bread
¼ cup hummus
½ ripe avocado, sliced
2 lettuce leaves
2 tablespoons basil pesto

Spread two slices of bread with 2 tablespoons hummus and then top with thin slices of avocado and a piece of lettuce. Spread 1 tablespoon of pesto on the two remaining pieces of bread. Put the sandwiches together, cut them into quarters, and add them to the serving plate.

WATERMELON CUPS

8 (8-ounce) clear plastic cups
8 plastic spoons
2 quarts of watermelon cubes

Divide the watermelon pieces among the cups and chill until serving time.

CUPCAKE CONES

Make the batter for Yellow Cake with Raspberry Filling (page 148). When ready to bake, place flat-bottomed ice cream cones in a muffin tin so they will not tip while baking. Fill the cones two-thirds full with cake batter; note that you won't need the whole amount, so have a small pan standing by and make yourself a mini cake!

Bake according to the cupcake directions. Frost or decorate to suit the occasion.

FISH STICKS WITH FRIENDS

Did some friends just drop by unannounced? This easy meal is perfect for last-minute guests. Keep an assembled apple galette (an easy-to-make open-faced apple tart) in the freezer so you can just pull it out and bake it to make this meal a breeze.

Crispy Fish Strips with Dipping Sauce (page 116)
Tartar Sauce (page 97)
Creamy Coleslaw (page 60)
French bread
Apple Galette (page 178)

CHICKEN WITH THE COUSINS

Plan some board games or card games for all ages to play before enjoying this easy meal. Everything can be prepared before the guests arrive.

Baked Chicken Strips (page 118) with Honey-Mustard Sauce (page 101)
Oven-Browned Potato Wedges (recipe follows)
Sliced tomatoes and cucumbers

French bread
Ice Cream Parfaits (page 192)

OVEN-BROWNED POTATO WEDGES

Serves 6

2 pounds medium red or Yukon gold potatoes
¾ teaspoon garlic salt
½ teaspoon freshly ground pepper
1½ tablespoons olive oil
½ teaspoon dried thyme

Preheat the oven to 400 degrees. Halve or quarter the potatoes and place them in a baking pan that will hold them in one layer. Sprinkle the garlic salt and pepper over the potatoes and drizzle the olive oil on top. Toss the potatoes with a spatula to coat with the oil and seasoning.

Roast for about 25 minutes, stirring twice. Sprinkle with the thyme and continue cooking for another 10 minutes, or until the potatoes are browned and soft in the centers. If making ahead, reheat in a 425-degree oven for 5 to 7 minutes until warm.

FAMILY BARBECUE NIGHT

*Gather the family together for a summer barbecue and
some time to talk about each one's summer activities.
End the meal with s'mores and your favorite songs.*

Pickles, carrots, and celery sticks with Spinach-Dill Dip (recipe follows)
Grilled Bratwurst Sausages with Mustards (recipe follows)
Spicy Turkey Burgers (recipe follows)
Macaroni Salad (page 62)

Fruit Skewers (page 201)
S'mores (recipe follows)

SPINACH-DILL DIP

Makes 2 cups

¾ cup eggless mayonnaise
¾ cup low-fat sour cream
2 cups chopped fresh spinach leaves
2 cloves garlic, finely minced
Freshly ground pepper
¼ cup fresh dill, or 2 teaspoons dried dill

Add all ingredients to the bowl of a blender or food processor and blend until smooth. Pour into a serving bowl, then cover and chill for 1 hour before serving with an assortment of prepared raw veggies.

GRILLED BRATWURST SAUSAGES WITH MUSTARDS

Serves 6

4 to 6 bratwurst sausages
1 cup beer (optional)
2 tablespoons olive oil (optional)
Whole-grain mustard
French's mustard, or other yellow mustard
Colman's mustard, or other spicy mustard

Stovetop method: Place the sausages in one layer in a heavy skillet. Pour in the beer and drizzle the olive oil over the top of the sausages. Cook over medium heat, turning to brown evenly until they reach 160 degrees in the center. (The beer will evaporate during cooking and should be about gone by the time the sausages are done. This, along with the olive oil, will cling to the brats, creating a flavorful coating.) Serve hot, with mustards on the side.

Grill method: Prick the sausages 4 to 5 times with a fork and place on a preheated grill. Turn after 5 minutes and continue to cook until well browned. Check with a meat thermometer and take off the grill when they reach 160 degrees in the center. Serve hot, with the mustards on the side.

SPICY TURKEY BURGERS

Serves 6

2 pounds ground turkey
3 tablespoons grated yellow onion
2 cloves garlic, minced
1 tablespoon Worcestershire sauce
1 teaspoon cumin
1 teaspoon paprika
6 slices sharp cheddar cheese (optional)
Eggless mayonnaise, lettuce, and pickle, for garnish
6 hamburger buns
Burger Sauce (page 100)

Combine the turkey, onion, garlic, Worcestershire, cumin, and paprika in a medium bowl. Mix well with wet hands and shape into 6 patties, leaving the centers thinner so the burgers will cook evenly.

Spray a heavy skillet, large enough to hold the 6 patties without crowding, with cooking oil and preheat it over medium-high heat. Cook the patties for 5 to 6 minutes, then flip them over with a spatula. Continue to cook for another 5 to 6 minutes until no longer soft in the middle, adding the cheese during the last 2 minutes.

Spread mayonnaise on the bottom half of each bun and top with lettuce and pickle. Place a patty on top and finish with a spoonful of Burger Sauce. Cover with the top half of the bun and serve.

S'MORES

This recipe makes 6 s'mores, but you'll probably want to double it!

Serves 6

1 (3-ounce) milk chocolate bar, broken into 6 pieces
6 graham cracker sheets, broken into 12 halves
6 eggless marshmallows

Place 1 square of chocolate on a graham cracker half. Toast a marshmallow over a fire or cook in the microwave for 15 to 20 seconds. Slide the marshmallow onto the graham cracker with the chocolate. Top with a second graham cracker square, and press the "sandwich" together gently. Cool slightly before eating.

BUILD-A-PIZZA PARTY

This party always ends up being a great time for kids and adults alike. Set bowls of the toppings out on the counter along with a stack of flour tortillas in a basket. The adults will join right in once they see how much fun the kids are having.

Assorted veggies with guacamole (purchase your favorite brand)
Build-a-Pizzas (recipe follows)
Watermelon Wedges
Peanut Butter Cookies (page 132)
Refrigerator Sugar Cookies (page 128)

BUILD-A-PIZZAS

The following proportions are for 1 single pizza serving:
1 (8-inch) flour tortilla
3 tablespoons spaghetti or pizza sauce

2 to 3 toppings of choice (suggestions follow)
½ teaspoon spaghetti seasoning (optional)
½ cup mozzarella or cheese of choice, shredded

TOPPING SUGGESTIONS

Chopped or thin slices of pepperoni
Chopped ham
Drained, crushed pineapple
Sliced black olives
Chopped zucchini
Chopped tomatoes
Sliced or chopped mushrooms, cooked or raw
Crumbled, cooked, and drained sausage meat
Chopped red pepper
Chopped onion
Chopped fresh basil
Artichoke hearts, drained and sliced
Bacon bits

Preheat the oven to 425 degrees.

Place a tortilla on a large plate. Spread the spaghetti sauce evenly over the entire tortilla. Sprinkle your toppings of choice evenly over the sauce, then sprinkle with the spaghetti seasoning and the cheese. Slide the tortilla onto an individual pizza pan or bake several at a time on a baking sheet.

Place the pizza pan or baking sheet on the middle rack of the oven and bake for 13 to 15 minutes, or until the cheese is just melted and the edges have begun to brown slightly. Remove from the oven and cut into quarters with scissors or a pizza wheel. Make sure to cool the pizza enough so it doesn't burn young chefs' mouths.

COOK'S NOTE

- You can substitute English muffin halves for the tortillas; just use half the amount of sauce and toppings for two halves.

SODA FOUNTAIN PARTY AFTER THE MOVIES

Enjoy ice cream sodas and sundaes while you compare thoughts about the evening's movie.

Ice Cream Sodas, Ice Cream Sundaes, Italian Sodas, and Banana Splits (recipes follow)
Refrigerator Sugar Cookies (page 128)
Raspberry Bars (page 138)

ICE CREAM SODAS

These are best served in tall glasses with long-handled spoons and straws for sucking up every last bit of sweetness!

Serves 6

1 quart eggless vanilla ice cream
1 (2-quart) bottle soda water, cola, root beer, lemonade, or soda of choice
Sweetened whipped cream
6 maraschino cherries (optional)

Place 1 scoop of ice cream in a tall glass and add ½ cup of the soda water, cola, root-beer, lemonade, or other soda of your choice. Stir to partially mix the ice cream with the soda. Fill the glass to 1 inch from the top with soda. Top with a second scoop of ice cream, a spoonful of whipped cream, and a cherry. Repeat for the other 5 sodas. Place straws and long spoons in the glasses and serve.

ICE CREAM SUNDAES

Anything can go on top of a few scoops of ice cream. Use the suggestions below or come up with your own. How creative can you be?

Serves 6

1½ quarts eggless vanilla ice cream
1½ cups topping, such as chocolate, caramel, or strawberry sauce
⅓ cup chopped toasted nuts (optional)
Sweetened whipped cream
6 maraschino cherries

Here are a few additional suggestions for unique flavor combinations:

Peach ice cream topped with raspberry sauce
Chocolate ice cream topped with mint fudge sauce
Mango sorbet topped with chopped candied ginger
Lemon sorbet topped with drained crushed pineapple and sweetened with a little
    brown sugar

ITALIAN SODAS

Serves 6

The Italian soda actually originated in America, using Italian fruit flavorings. It is a soft drink made from carbonated water and simple syrup, often cherry or blackberry. When cream is added, it is called either a French soda or an Italian cream soda.

1 cup plus 2 tablespoons Italian syrup of choice
Crushed ice
1 (2-quart) bottle soda water

½ cup half-and-half (optional)
Sweetened whipped cream

Pour 3 tablespoons of syrup into each tall 24-ounce glass. Fill each glass halfway with crushed ice, then add the soda water to 1 inch from the top of the glass. Stir, then add a splash of half-and-half, if making a French soda. Top with whipped cream. Serve with a straw.

CLASSIC BANANA SPLIT

Serves 1

*The first banana split was made in 1904 by a
pharmacist at a drugstore lunch counter in Latrobe,
Pennsylvania. He was obviously on to a good thing!*

1 banana, halved lengthwise
1 scoop each of 3 different eggless ice cream flavors, preferably vanilla, strawberry,
  and chocolate
1 tablespoon each of chocolate sauce, sugared crushed strawberries, caramel sauce,
  marshmallow crème, or any dessert sauce of choice
3 tablespoons sweetened whipped cream
Crushed Oreos, mini marshmallows, chopped peanuts, mini chocolate chips, or
  crushed vanilla cookies, for topping
1 maraschino cherry

Place the split banana in a long dessert dish and top with the ice cream. Next, spoon a different sauce on each scoop of ice cream. Top each scoop with a little whipped cream and a sprinkling of your choice of topping. Finish with the cherry on the center scoop and serve immediately.

EGG ALERT: Check the marshmallow crème for possible eggs.

RESOURCES AND INFORMATION

EGG SUBSTITUTES

COMMERCIAL POWDERED EGG REPLACERS

Ener-G Egg Replacer and Bob's Red Mill Egg Replacer are generally available in super-markets and health-food stores, although there are other companies that produce fine egg-replacing products (see page 228 for more on how to order these products). Each brand of egg replacer works a little differently in recipes; no one is the overall best for all baking.

A simple guideline for egg substitutes is to replace no more than 1 egg per 1 cup of flour in baked goods; if a recipe calls for more eggs than that, it is best to look for an alternate recipe.

HOW TO USE A FEW COMMERCIAL EGG REPLACERS

The following egg replacer products will replace one egg.

1½ teaspoons Ener-G Egg Replacer, whisked with 2 tablespoons water until foamy	Add immediately to recipe.
1 tablespoon Bob's Red Mill Egg Replacer, whisked with 3 tablespoons water until well blended	This replacer seems to have more thickening power, and is suitable for meat dishes and casseroles. Add with the other liquid(s).
2 teaspoons Orgran No Egg Egg Replacer, whisked with 2 tablespoons water until well blended	Add with the other liquid(s).

XANTHAN GUM

Xanthan gum, not an egg replacer per se, is a commercial binder that adds moisture and stability to baked goods, and it reduces the crumbly texture of eggless cakes and muffins. Xanthan gum is found in many everyday products like salad dressings and breads, so it is not unique to eggless cooking. It only takes a little to change the texture, so the following chart is a suggested guideline for adding it to any recipe.

General Rule: ¼ to ½ teaspoon xanthan gum per 1 cup of flour	
Pancakes	½ teaspoon xanthan gum per 2 cups of flour
Muffins	¾ teaspoon xanthan gum per 12 muffins
Cakes	½ teaspoon xanthan gum per 2 cups of flour
Quick and Yeast Breads	¾ to 1 teaspoon xanthan gum per 4-by-9-inch loaf
Scones	¾ teaspoon xanthan gum per 12 scones

KITCHEN PANTRY EGG REPLACERS

The following ordinary kitchen ingredients will replace one egg.

Replacer	Additional instructions	Use for
1 teaspoon baking powder, mixed into the flour in the recipe	Add 2 tablespoons water to the liquids	Pancakes, muffins, cookies, and cakes.
2 tablespoons unsweetened applesauce (reduce other liquid by 1 tablespoon)	Add ½ teaspoon baking powder to the flour	Muffins, cookies, and breads. The product will be a little denser than those made with just a powdered egg replacer.
2 tablespoons mashed ripe banana	Add ½ teaspoon baking powder to the flour	Pancakes and muffins (it will make them moister). Check that the banana flavor is compatible.
1 tablespoon unflavored gelatin, dissolved into 1 tablespoon cold water		Add immediately to pâtés and meatloaves at the time other liquids are added.
¼ cup silken tofu, well blended with ½ teaspoon baking powder		Dense or moist baked products except cakes.
1 tablespoon cornstarch, whisked with 3 tablespoons water		Sauces that are to be thickened just before serving.
½ teaspoon baking soda, mixed into 2 tablespoons buttermilk (mixture will become foamy)		Mix together and add with liquids; use in muffins and pancakes.
2 tablespoons carbonated water, mixed into 2 teaspoons flour		Add to bread and cookie dough with other liquid(s).

PASTRY AND BREAD GLAZES

These glazes, used instead of an egg wash, will make baked goods shiny.

Substitute for egg wash	How to apply	What it does
¼ cup of light corn syrup thinned with ¼ teaspoon hot water	Brush on top of baked breads as they come out of the oven	Creates a sweet-tasting egg-wash shine on bread crusts and pies.
1½ tablespoons melted butter	Brush on top of baked breads as they come out of the oven	Creates an egg-wash shine on bread crusts.
1 to 1½ tablespoons whipping cream	Brush on top of piecrusts just before baking	Makes a nice glaze on the baked pastry.

HIDDEN EGGS

Eggs—especially egg whites—are not always easily recognized in food. The following chart lists a variety of foods and products that may or most likely contain some form of egg. If the word "vegan" is used on the label, you can be assured the product does not contain egg in any form.

Product	Form of Egg
Artificial crab and lobster	Egg white is used as a binder; the product is called surimi or kamaboko.
Bakery mixes	Cakes, muffins, waffles, and bread mixes may contain powdered egg, even if the directions also call for adding fresh egg. Manufacturers change ingredients and labels without notice!

Bakery products	Breads and pastries often contain egg, and even if they don't, their top surfaces are very often glazed with an egg-wash mixture for shine or to help sprinkles, seeds, and such to adhere.
Baking powder biscuits	Though biscuits can be made without egg, it may be added to the basic recipe to make the biscuits lighter.
Bar drinks	Foamy specialty bar drinks (like a gin fizz) may contain powdered egg white.
Batter-fried and breaded foods	A mixture of diluted egg helps the breading stick to meat or vegetables when frying. Tempura and fish and chips are good examples. Fried chicken and croquettes are also usually dipped in a thick egg batter.
Bockwurst sausage	This veal sausage is often bound with egg white.
Breakfast at cafés and restaurants	Small and large restaurants often cook the eggs and breakfast meats on the same grill and use the same utensils for dishes with egg and eggless dishes.
Cakes and cookies	Almost all cakes and cookies made outside the home kitchen contain egg, unless they are prepared in a special egg-free bakery. If the product looks yellowish, there is a good chance it contains whole eggs.
Candy	Egg whites are used in some special candy varieties such as divinity, candied sugared nuts, and sea foam candy.
Cheese fondue	Egg can be used to bind the cheese and liquids.
Consommé and other clear, hot liquids	Gourmet chefs sometimes add whipped egg whites to the finished strained broth to help collect particles for a clearer soup. Old-fashioned boiled coffee can be prepared with eggshells to make the coffee clearer.
Cosmetics and shampoos	A few brands contain egg for richness.
"Egg Beaters" egg white products	This product is a low-cholesterol form of egg sold in the dairy section; its primary ingredient is egg white.

Fried rice	Strips of cooked egg are usually added before the dish is served. When placing your order, ask to have your serving prepared in a clean sauté pan and served without egg.
Frostings and fillings	Whipped egg white makes frostings light and fluffy. Eggs are added to almost all cake fillings, including chocolate, lemon, nut, and butterscotch ones.
Garden products	Some sprays or small pellets used to discourage the presence of rabbits, gophers, and other small animals use egg as a binder.
Gluten-free products	Breads, piecrusts, cookies, pizza dough, pasta, and crackers may contain egg white to make the product light or hold together better.
Horseradish	Some brands of plain prepared horseradish, in addition to most creamy styles, contain egg yolks. Kosher-style horseradish does not have egg.
Marshmallows	Most packaged marshmallows do not contain eggs; however, marshmallow fluff sold in a jar contains egg white.
Meatloaves and meatballs	Those sold in the frozen food section often do not contain egg; however, homemade meatballs and those served in restaurants usually do have eggs in them.
Medications and vaccinations	Some vaccines are cultured in egg, so check with your health provider before receiving a preventive inoculation.
Panko flakes (Japanese bread crumbs)	A few brands contain egg white.
Pasta, fresh and dried	All fresh pastas contain egg, as do some brands of dried specialty pastas such as fettuccine, no-boil lasagna strips, and pappardelle.
Pies and tarts	The top crusts of pies and tarts are often glazed with an egg wash before baking for shine.

Potatoes	Scalloped potatoes and mashed potatoes may have egg added, particularly in restaurants, so the product will hold up for an extended serving time.
Power drinks and smoothies	Some add powders that are enriched with egg.
Rice cakes	Most Quaker-brand cakes contain egg white; many other brands are egg-free.
Salad dressings	Mayonnaise, egg white, or whole egg may be added to salad dressings to give them more body (Caesar dressing is a prime example).
Sorbet or sherbet	Fruit sorbet is usually made without eggs or milk, but sherbet most often contains milk and/or eggs.
Stir-fried meats and fish	Meat and fish may be dipped in a light egg-white coating to enhance browning.
Stuffing for meats and poultry	Many restaurant and home cooks use egg as a binder when preparing stuffing.
Sweet hot mustard/Chinese mustard	Some brands use egg yolk as a thickener.
Tacos, mini frozen	José Olé frozen mini beef and cheese tacos contain egg; however, many brands of frozen tacos are eggless.
Tempura	Vegetables and seafood are dipped in a light egg batter before deep-frying.
Waffles and pancakes	Restaurant servings always contain eggs, and most mixes contain dried egg even if they also require a fresh egg to be added.

EGGS BY A DIFFERENT NAME

Since January 1, 2006, the FDA has required food products to be clearly labeled if they contain egg or other allergens. However, there are a number of products that are exempt from this labeling law. For this reason, it is very important to read each label very carefully to identify egg ingredients or derivatives. Egg in different forms is an important emulsifier that is widely used in the food industry.

Cosmetics, prescriptions, over-the-counter medications, pet food, garden products, and craft materials are exempt from this new ruling, but may contain forms of egg white or yolk. Again, read carefully!

Albumin	An egg-white protein that can be in a dried form and is water soluble.
Diprivan	The brand name for Propofol, a form of anesthetic. Those with an egg allergy may be sensitive to this medication.
Kollimex	An egg-white powder that improves the texture of Asian noodles.
Lecithin	Most lecithin is derived from soy, but it can come from eggs. It may be used in medicines as well as food products.
Phosvitin	The protein compound of egg yolk can be used as an emulsifier; this is a brand name for it.
Propofol	See Diprivan above
Simplesse	An egg-protein product that can be used as a fat substitute in low-calorie foods.
SKM Egg products	This egg product made from dried whole eggs can be found in biscuits, cakes, dressings, and meat products.

PRODUCT SOURCES

The following are good resources for ingredients used in eggless cooking as well as for eggless products.

EGG REPLACERS

Egg replacer, baking mixes
Ener-G Foods, Inc.
5960 1st Avenue South
Seattle, WA 98108
1-800-331-5222
www.ener-g.com

Egg replacer, specialty flours, and baking mixes
Bob's Red Mill Natural Foods, Inc.
13521 SE Pheasant Court
Milwaukie, OR 97222
www.bobsredmill.com

Egg replacer, baking mixes, and pastas without other allergens
Orgran Natural Foods
Brewster, NY
www.orgran.com

EGGLESS MAYONNAISES

There are many good commercial eggless mayonnaises available on the market. Each one has a slightly different flavor and consistency. You can use them right from the jar or adjust the seasonings to taste. I find that a splash of fresh lemon juice, a very small dollop of Dijon mustard, and a grinding of black pepper add extra zest.

This is my favorite eggless mayonnaise; it's zesty and makes a wonderful base for all mayonnaise dressings and sauces. It is available in the refrigerator section of most markets.
Wildwood Aioli
www.wildwoodfoods.com

There are several different varieties to choose from; the organic style with the green lid is my first choice.
Follow Your Heart Vegenaise
www.followyourheart.com

This is a basic mayonnaise that is easily found on supermarket shelves alongside egg mayonnaises; it comes in a choice of container sizes.
Spectrum Organic Mayonnaise
www.spectrumorganics.com

EGGLESS COOKIES

Just a few of the eggless cookies on the market are listed below. New products are being introduced all the time and can be found online.

Cookies without eggs and nuts
Alice's Stick Cookies
www.alicesstickcookies.com

Eggless cookies
MI-DEL/Panos Brands
www.midelcookies.com

Eggless, wheat-free cookies and recipes
Simply Shari's
www.simplysharis.com

Cookie and cake mixes
Cherry Brook Kitchen
www.cherrybrookkitchen.com

Egg- and dairy-free baked goods and treats
Divvies Products
www.divvies.com

Eggless lemon shortbread and gluten- and allergen-free mixes
Pamela's Products, Inc.
www.pamelasproducts.com

Eggless gingersnaps and other allergen-free products
Annie's Homegrown
www.annies.com

USEFUL BOOKS ABOUT COOKING AND FOOD ALLERGIES

Learn more about managing food allergies and living without eggs.

The Allergy Sourcebook, Zellerbach, Merla, Lowell House, Los Angeles, 2000.

> The text includes information about why allergies exist, airborne allergies, and allergies to substances other than food.

Allergy-Free Cookbook, Sherwood, Alice, DK Publishing, New York, 2009.

> This is a good cookbook for a person with allergies to nuts, eggs, and wheat.

Bakin' Without Eggs, Emro, Rosemarie, St. Martin's Griffin, New York, 1999.

Many innovative recipes for muffins, cakes, desserts, and specialty foods.

Cooking Free, Fenster, Carol, PhD, Avery, New York, 2005.

Great resource for a number of food-related health issues presented in excellent chart form, as well as recipes for all types of meals.

The Divvies Bakery Cookbook, Sandler, Lori, St. Martin's Press, New York, 2010.

Many recipes for eggless cupcakes, cookies, and desserts, along with party decorating ideas.

Food Allergies, Taylor-Butler, Christine, Children's Press, Scholastic, Inc., New York, 2008.

An informative little book to help a child understand all aspects of food allergies.

Food Allergies and Children, a Pocket Guide for Parents, Trone, Julie.

A good information source for anyone new to food allergies.

Food Allergies for Dummies, Wood, Robert A., MD, Wiley Publishing, Inc., Indianapolis, 2007.

Hard-to-find answers to many questions about food allergies are presented here in an entertaining and helpful way.

Food Allergy Cookbook, Bruce-Gardyne, Lucinda, Reader's Digest, Pleasantville, 2008.

Most recipes give suggestions for substitutions when more than one allergen must be avoided.

The Food Allergy Mama's Baking Book, Kelly, Rudnicki, Agate Publishing, Evanston, 2009.

Provides an excellent section on tips for cooking without eggs, dairy, and nuts, plus good recipes for baked goods.

Living Without, a bimonthly publication for people with allergies and food sensitivities. LivingWithout.com, 1-800-381-1288.

Real Food for Healthy Kids, Seaman, Tracey and Steel, Tanya Wenman, HarperCollins Publishers, New York, 2008.

> This is a kid-approved cookbook with great healthy food for all kids with many recipes that can be adapted to eggless.

Taking Food Allergies to School, Weiner, Ellen, The Guidance Group, Virtual Help, Inc., Woodbury, NY 2012.

> A story about a child's willpower and what happens when you have an allergic reaction.

Understanding and Managing Your Child's Food Allergy, Sicherer, Scott, MD, The John Hopkins Press, Baltimore, 2006.

> A pediatric food specialist gives good insight to parents of children with food allergies.

The Whole Foods Allergy Cookbook, Pascal, Cybele, Square One Publishers, Garden City Park, 2009.

> This is a complete cookbook with recipes for everything from baked goods to vegetables and after-school treats, all the while keeping food allergies in mind.

ONLINE ARTICLES AND INFORMATION

In addition to the food company websites listed on pages 228 to 230, these are good online resources for those with egg allergies.

www.allergyeats.com. A searchable guide to allergy-friendly restaurants across the country

www.allergyfreepassport.com. Worldwide travel allergy-free resource for food translations, alert cards, and more

www.allergyfreetable.com. Helpful information for many phases of food allergies

www.allergykids.com. Help for kids at school, plus allergy information

www.chefs2be.com. Ideas for cooking classes for kids

www.egglesscooking.com. Egg-free recipes and suggestions

www.faankids.org. Website just for kids with allergies

www.fda.gov/food. Information on all phases of food allergies including recalls, ingredients, allergens, and food alerts

www.foodallergy.org. Food Allergy and Anaphylaxis Network (FAAN) has information about allergies in general, plus details about food allergies, treatment, and resources

www.mayoclinic.com. Food allergy and food intolerance information

www.safetysack.com. Pouches for kids' allergy medications

www.singleswithfoodallergies.com. Dating and social relationships with others with allergies

INDEX

ACKNOWLEDGMENTS

Many thanks to my support team of wonderful and talented friends, family, and professionals who helped me create *Eating Eggless*. I am most grateful for their advice and encouragement during all stages of writing and production.

Granddaughters Meghan Mannes and Elizabeth Monroe guided me through the whole project with their perspective, computer expertise, good advice, and enthusiastic knowledge of food.

Lana Staheli, PhD and author, was my consultant and chief motivator, offering suggestions and useful resources as well as being a taster. Lynn Staheli, MD and author, helped with initial contacts and resources.

Barbara Cairns did extensive editorial work as the book began to develop, and Janet Daggett never allowed me to lose track of my goal; she provided me with numerous creative resources.

During the early phase of the project, Deborah Cughan worked through the first steps with me, while Nikki Whittle, Matthew Ahl, and Sue Draper helped launch the project.

Thank you to John and Jan at Cooking in Madison Park, Seattle. Their suggestions were most helpful, and their store has all of the cooking necessities and more. In addition, they have a wonderful selection of linens and table appointments that were perfect for staging my food photography.

Lindsey Denman professionally staged and photographed many foods. Jeff Larson was proofreader before the production phase. Lisa Gordanier gave me constructive editorial input and directed me to Girl Friday Productions. Initial social media expertise was provided by Shawn Filer and Meghan Mannes.

It was this team that made the book happen, along with the following people who tasted dishes, provided their objective views, and contributed in many other ways: Mary Ellen Denman, Pat Donahoe, Pat and Frank Kerr, Foff Myers, Delphine Campbell, Kay Larson, George Campbell, Diane Curtis, Marcia Lewis, Christine and Bill Campbell, Diane Moxness, and other friends.

A special word of appreciation goes to the staff of Girl Friday Productions, especially editors Meghan Harvey and Emilie Sandoz-Voyer.

ABOUT THE AUTHOR

Photograph © 2014 Ingrid Pape-Sheldon

Elizabeth Moody Campbell is an advocate for food safety. She helped sponsor the first Food Allergy Educator Symposium at Seattle Children's Hospital, and her support has helped develop educational programs about food allergies.

19591307R00154

Printed in Great Britain
by Amazon